The Econosphere

The Econosphere

What Makes the Economy Really
Work, How to Protect It, and
Maximize Your Opportunity for
Financial Prosperity

Craig Thomas

Vice President, Publisher: Tim Moore
Associate Publisher and Director of Marketing: Amy Neidlinger
Executive Editor: Jeanne Glasser
Editorial Assistant: Myesha Graham
Development Editor: Russ Hall
Operations Manager: Gina Kanouse
Senior Marketing Manager: Julie Phifer
Publicity Manager: Laura Czaja
Assistant Marketing Manager: Megan Colvin
Cover Designer: Alan Clements
Managing Editor: Kristy Hart
Project Editor: Anne Goebel
Copy Editor: Apostrophe Editing Services
Proofreader: Kathy Ruiz
Indexer: Erika Millen
Senior Compositor: Jake McFarland
Manufacturing Buyer: Dan Uhrig

© 2010 by Pearson Education, Inc.
Publishing as FT Press
Upper Saddle River, New Jersey 07458

Printed in the United States of America
First Printing November 2009

ISBN-10: 0-13-701998-X
ISBN-13: 978-0-13-701998-4

Pearson Education LTD.
Pearson Education Australia PTY, Limited.
Pearson Education Singapore, Pte. Ltd.
Pearson Education North Asia, Ltd.
Pearson Education Canada, Ltd.
Pearson Educación de Mexico, S.A. de C.V.
Pearson Education—Japan
Pearson Education Malaysia, Pte. Ltd.

Library of Congress Cataloging-in-Publication Data
Thomas, Craig, 1969-
   The econosphere : what makes the economy really work, how to protect it, and maximize your opportunity for financial prosperity/Craig Thomas.
      p. cm.
   ISBN 978-0-13-701998-4 (hbk. : alk. paper) 1. Economics. 2. Economics–Sociological aspects.   I. Title.
   HB171.T495 2010
   330–dc22
                                                            2009027932

To Heidi, who has patiently endured the verbal monologue version of this book for the past 19 years. I love you.

Contents

Acknowledgments

I would like to acknowledge the contributions of Gerald and Leanne Sindell of Thought Leaders International in helping make this book a reality. I would also like to acknowledge those people who have over the years granted me more than enough rope with which to hang myself: Paul Getman, Mark Zandi, Ray Torto, Bill Wheaton, and Joe Azrack.

About the Author

Craig Thomas has worked as an economist in the private sector for the past fifteen years. Specializing in regional, macro, and real estate economics, Mr. Thomas has held the posts of senior economist and director at Citigroup, CB Richard Ellis/Torto Wheaton Research, and Economy.com. Over the years, Mr. Thomas has modeled and analyzed markets and asset classes around the globe and has presented his work throughout Europe, Asia, and North America.

Prior to this, Mr. Thomas completed his graduate and undergraduate studies at the University of Maine, Orono. While there he studied and gained degrees in economics, with concentrations in agriculture and resource economics, and business.

While writing this book, Mr. Thomas split his time between Manhattan and Nahant, Massachusetts.

Preface

When the economy is not giving us the messages that we want to hear, we tend to think of it as broken, unfair, and maybe even a little malicious. Someone ought to step in and fix it or adjust it, just like the government has tried to do now and again. But if the economy is actually a self-sustaining social ecosystem, the same way our physical ecosystem is, perhaps it is better-suited to take care of itself, and our tinkering with it might disrupt instead of help it.

In *The Econosphere*, you finally will understand the laws that govern our financial world—the everyday world of work and play; planning, saving, and investing; and the economic considerations for everything that comprises our daily lives. This is a world that is a most fundamental aspect of everything that we are, and we need to understand it clearly to make intelligent choices. Here, I show you that we are living, breathing, and working within the self-regulating, holistic Econosphere whether we know it or not.

You will understand why others' wealth neither hurts nor benefits you. You will understand what fairness is in an economic sense. And you will see clearly how to make the most of your time and labor.

1

Born with a Loaf of Bread

How the World Prospers

My grandmother, the late Althea Thomas of Kunkle, Pennsylvania, had a saying, "Every baby is born with a loaf of bread." She would say this to comfort someone expecting a new addition to the family who was perhaps worrying about family finances. I suppose the phrase would be the antidote to the less comforting, "One more mouth to feed." I think it's a nice saying; it's soothing and optimistic. Oddly, it has stuck in my head from the first day that I heard it repeated, and I have long wondered why that is. In fact, there is much more to that old adage than just kind, matriarchal reassurance.

It is a wonderful saying because it is absolutely true. And if everyone could just understand that one fact, I think the world would be such a happier, more serene and certainly better managed place for all of us to live. The saying actually goes to the heart of how it is that our economic world can support its billions of inhabitants as well as it does. It can because new inhabitants bring with them the basic raw materials to support themselves and those they care about throughout an entire lifetime—and in some cases, even produce far more than they ultimately need, which brings us to...

The First Law of the Econosphere

The Law of Growth:
Unless purposefully hindered, each new person brings additional wealth to the world.

We All Share the Same Goal: Maximize Happiness

I call the environment in which we live the *Econosphere*. It is the world created by and governing of human decision making, and it is our home. It provides for us and nurtures us. It reacts to and informs our every interaction and, if we understand it, allows us to optimize the use of our life spans moment by moment. This environment is not, however, one made of oxygen and hydrogen, oil and steel, high mountains and low plains. Rather, the Econosphere is our *social* environment, where we work, live, raise our families, and govern ourselves. We need to start thinking about the economy as a holistic, natural system. Think for a moment about the biosphere, its makeup and its importance in sustaining life. Scientists study our complex biosphere in incredible detail, employing all kinds of technologies to understand how it sustains us. Most of us generally accept that the biosphere provides the air we breathe and thus we need to care for it by not overwhelming its capability to renew itself with harmful chemical emissions, heat, and dust. It is the biological part of our environment, and our environment needs to be protected.

What about our social environment? Should we make the same efforts to study and protect our Econosphere? The answer is an emphatic yes! Unfortunately, many people see the economy as simply the outcome of public policy, a collection of opaque statistics, or even a term that describes how much money we are or are not making, saving, or investing. But we generally do not see the economy as a natural system that nurtures and sustains us.

Now, you might be asking what is so perfect and balancing about the economy? Its fits and starts, enormous perceived inequities, and even its seemingly cruel nature give it the reputation of being far from perfect. However, consider what it does for us. On a planet that is home to billions, the Econosphere signals to each of us what needs to be conserved by assigning a market price that is dear. In that same vein, if the price of something is high relative the cost to create it, the Econosphere signals us to put our efforts into supplying more of this thing. On the opposite end of spectrum, if we have too much of one thing, the Econosphere devalues it so that we consume more or produce less of it.

And there are rewards for good behavior; the more productive we are in producing what it is that our fellow inhabitants crave, the more we are rewarded. If we produce great value, we subsequently can consume things of great value or save our earnings to share with those whom we love. Moreover, like a great coach, the Econosphere motivates us through intense competition to be innovative. The more we innovate, the more we are rewarded; but even better, the more we innovate, the better off we all are because the products and services that we create for our fellow people are ever superior to those that came before. This is what allows us to increase the quality of all our lives over time and allows this small world to make room for all those on its surface.

To those who are inclined to see it, it is breathtaking choreography on a global scale with billions of performers, each one in character, playing his or her unique role so that the entire ensemble shines. The Econosphere provides *for* us, yet it is also *of* us.

Where we do find areas of our social environment that are tarnished and polluted, we also always see a visible interfering human hand. Where there is hunger, there is typically not a lack of food, but rather a closed border, a cruel authoritarian regime, or a captive market not allowed to assign prices or incent production. Where there is poverty, we often find bigotry and artificial castes maintained by brutal rule. Where we see inefficiency and waste, we typically find central planning, public ownership, and favored status. Even in our recent financial crisis, complicit in the mistakes made by lenders, borrowers, and investors is the hand of the central-planner. In this case, public policy subsidizing the purchase of homes via tax breaks and loose borrowing standards had their start in the

Clinton Administration's fixation on increasing the home-ownership rate and the Bush Administration's willingness to carry that torch with its promotion of an *ownership society*—apparently ownership at any cost!

Fortunately, like someone trying to stop the grass from growing by stamping on it, efforts to rob us of our natural social environment are usually short-lived, eventually failing. Like plants sprouting through cracks in a sidewalk, the Econosphere finds ways to guide our lives even as some might work to pave it all over. Similarly, you always find a way to maximize your happiness, even within the confines of those impediments that might be thrown up in your path—it's just that maximum potential happiness is not as high when the Econosphere is not left to function unfettered.

Love and Protect Your Econosphere

If you understand the Econosphere, you can better protect it from harm, just as many seek to do with the biosphere. And when you understand its natural laws, you are much more likely to thrive within it because an understanding of the laws of the Econosphere cannot help but give you an advantage over others who, sadly, might believe that their lot in life is done *to* them, not *by* them. Understanding the Econosphere's functioning and rules can give you the ability to concentrate on where you can add the most value, improve your information so that you can make superior decisions, and to generally be at peace with a social environment that best serves your needs by being allowed to function naturally.

When you don't understand the forces at play in the world you're living in, anything and everything can be terrifying. But when you have the tools to properly understand and translate information as it comes to you, whether it is in understanding the pros and cons of a candidate's proposed public policy, why the job market functions as it does, why the marketplace prices goods and services higher or lower, or even why you make the life and work decisions that you make, there comes a peace of mind.

The Second Law of the Econosphere

The Law of Information:
In the Econosphere, no matter what the problem, better information is always part of the solution.

The Marketplace Is Perfect: It Is Information That Is Imperfect

It is not the functioning of the economy that creates adverse outcomes; rather it is poor or inadequate information and lack of understanding that causes you to make ill-advised and costly decisions.

If you manage to collect and decipher better information than is commonly available, there is a greater chance that the Econosphere can work better for you. It's not so much that you need to discover unique facts, but rather that if you can take the same information that others have in front of them and understand it all at a much higher level, discarding the noise and making better use of your understanding of the natural laws of the Econosphere, you can thrive.

Even among professional economists, quite a few cannot sort through the day's headlines and filter for themselves those events that are relevant to the economy from those that are a distraction, and then make the decisions that benefit their lives and the lives of their loved ones. If you don't understand the Econosphere, there is a likelihood you will lurch from headline to headline, grabbing hold with both hands every upturn and downturn in the news cycle. You will greet every statement with apprehension and will have little basis to judge the quality of every promise.

For instance, consider our recent economic problems, the roots of which took hold with the burst of speculative investing in housing starting in 2004. (The roots go deeper than that, specifically to the earlier-mentioned incentives created by public policy, but those are aside from the point I want to make here.)

Is there anything wrong with a house per se? No, houses are good things. So, what was the problem? Investors (both homebuyers and major institutions that secured or invested in the underlying mortgages) over-estimated future house price gains. Lenders under-estimated the risk in lending to households for the purpose of purchasing over-valued homes. Builders built too many homes, expecting demand to remain elevated. The problem was not that the market readily allows for the construction and purchase of homes. Rather, we had an information problem. Investors ignored housing affordability as an indicator for home values; builders lost track of basic demographic certainties; banks forgot the number one rule of banking—never lend to someone who really needs the money!

So, we ended up with a mess that spread well beyond housing to every facet of the global economy. And how do we get out of a mess like this? Investors that made poor investments need to accept their losses. Banks need to foreclose upon bad loans. Builders need to stop building houses.

What about all the emergency actions that were undertaken? Ultimately, the astounding array of new policies did not stop any of the inevitable pain, but did cost U.S. taxpayers billions while likely prolonging and spreading our problems. We can see now that by intermittently and unpredictably changing the rules of the game for businesses and households so that information became even more muddled, these measures likely increased the risks inherent in our decision making.

Would it have been worse had these new policies not been put in place? No one can say with any certainty because the Econosphere does not allow for do-overs. However, given that the mess only got worse even after the measures were put into place, we must conclude that the goals of the policies were not fulfilled. And this is not terribly surprising because none of these policies were done with any reverence to the natural functioning of the Econosphere. No matter how well intentioned they were, they never actually had a chance.

Along these same lines, we cannot help but wonder *what if* housing speculators and mortgage lenders (not to mention the FDIC, Federal Reserve, Congress, and whoever else might also act as an anointed public overseer) had better information before any of this had begun, it all could have been avoided. Better knowledge of and respect for the powerful natural laws of the Econosphere would have saved us a lot of time and headaches! We cannot improve the Econosphere anymore than we can improve upon the laws of physics, but we can improve information.

Just as in our physical environment, the rules and functioning of the economy are essentially constant, unaffected by our day-to-day considerations about our work, leisure, saving, and consumption. It is always unique or superior information that helps us make better decisions. And, even our choices in politics are one way we express our understanding of what harms or helps us within the Econosphere. In the same way that someone can avoid chemicals that harm the physical environment, you might also vote against a candidate who proposes policies that might impede the proper functioning of the economy by encouraging or discouraging certain kinds of production or consumption, or in adversely changing the way that the economy distributes scarce resources.

You Live in the Econosphere

Because economics is about making decisions, you must see your economic condition as a collection of actions—past and present—made by individuals to increase each individual's happiness. And you should not just see this as simply a product of consumerism or greed—many wonderful things make you happy that are not related to stereotypes of mindless consumption for-its-own-sake. Happiness can be derived from providing for your family, preserving free time to mentor young people, the pursuit of the arts, or the opportunity to engage in charitable activities. It's all the same, as long as it brings you happiness. Every day you decide what makes you happy, and you make decisions to achieve your goals with whatever information you can gather. You do this every second of every day that you are awake. (You even shape your sleeping habits to maximize your happiness as well!)

You are born to live in your environment; both a physical environment and a social environment. Your physical environment should be plainly obvious to you. It's the sun to warm you, air to breath, food to sustain you. Your social environment is mostly invisible, and the parts you encounter can seem chaotic and not particularly interconnected. Until you know what the rules are, it's going to be difficult to contemplate and enjoy the Econosphere. But whether you understand it or not, you are living in it. Just as you don't need to be an environmentalist to breathe air or drink water, you don't need to be an economist to function within the Econosphere and work to maximize your happiness. It's inborn.

Can You Be Green About Your Econosphere?

There is a great deal of cultural emphasis today in being "green," the belief that you are better off taking care to eat wholesome and nutritious food, minimize your negative impact on the physical environment you share with everyone, and generally become a better steward of those resources you use to sustain yourself. For instance, you might choose to eat organic foods because you believe that the chemical applications found in the production of conventional agriculture contributes to unwanted chemical runoff into our aquifers or perhaps even the buildup of such chemicals within your own body.

In choosing to be green, you use the information that you have in hand to make what you believe is the best decision for our physical environment and for yourself. That is not to say that you are correct, but each of us tries to employ the best information that we have and that we can gather to make the right decisions. In the instance of avoiding pesticides, you have gathered enough information to come to the conclusion that you can achieve the most happiness by buying and consuming organic food.

If you can see your choices regarding the physical environment that are intended to bring you happiness, you can then expand this understanding to the less well-understood realm of your social environment—the Econosphere. Of course, your decisions regarding your physical environment are in the realm of the Econosphere, as well. However, how you *choose* to work and consume as part of our economy can be a bit harder to see and appreciate. How you choose to use finite resources, whether clean water or your own life span, are economic decisions.

You automatically become more productive if you can receive and react to the incentives and disincentives provided within the Econosphere. If there is too much of one thing, the price goes down, and thus supply reacts by cutting production. If we have too little of a thing (gasoline), the price rises, some of us step in with more supply, or even create alternatives to that good or service.

You are optimally productive if you can react to market pricing, dedicate yourself to a task, and trade the goods and services you produce freely, seeking the best value for your effort. The more productive you are, the greater your collective wealth and well-being. Also, the more productive you are at work, the more opportunity you have to be at leisure, another key ingredient to maximizing happiness.

To these ends, you must receive signals from the economy as to the value of goods and services that you can produce to trade for others' goods and services. It is essential for your own good that you develop an appreciation of how the Econosphere works so that you see the information necessary for you to provide for yourself and your family and optimize the value that you bring by employing all the abilities and possibilities that come in the course of your life. It is really about understanding and appreciating the natural flow of this holistic system of interaction, so you can make good decisions in work and play to receive the full value implicit in your very existence, and second, not do anything to harm or impede the Econosphere's natural functioning. You are the steward of your environments, both physical and social.

Which brings us to...

The Third Law of the Econosphere

The Law of Sustainability:

The Econosphere's bounty comes from people and nothing else. The animating force of the Econosphere is humanity.

Because the Econosphere is the result of our work and our choices, the basic building block of the Econosphere is the human life span. Human energy is our basic raw material, not oil, gold, soil, or water. Sure, we do need a physical space to inhabit, but there is, nonetheless, no value creation or intrinsic worth without us. Thus, all economic worth radiates from the time *we* are afforded and those talents that *we* cultivate within each of us.

As an example, let's see why the economy is about us and not some commodity like oil. Oil in the ground is absolutely worthless. Oil without the combustion engine is worthless. Oil without people wanting transportation across long distances or to heat their homes or to generate power is worthless. It is only worth something if it is pumped to the surface, transported, refined, and eventually consumed.

That entire process is done with the consumption of human time and talent. Moreover, the extent to which that process is possible and optimally performed depends on whether inhabitants of the Econosphere are fully able to collaborate and trade with one another.

What the Econosphere does is create the signals, that is, market prices that prompt some people to see the need for oil and motivate them to find ways to extract, refine, and trade that oil for money with which to purchase goods and services to maximize happiness. The Econosphere provides the basic flow of information, incentives, and disincentives to guide each of our daily lives. Now, I use oil only as an example. The same analysis can be used in the production of bread, financial advice, music, or robots. None of the raw materials that go into the production of such goods and services is worth anything without the essential ingredient: the human life span.

Let's look at the natural process of our lives. First, most people are born with the essential capacities to provide their sustenance—though we should acknowledge that for those who are oppressed within command economies or in societies where bigotry bars some groups from education or certain vocations, such people might never live up to their potential. Yet, even acknowledging that some in this world are held back by the hand of another, it is never a question of slicing up a pie made up of all the wealth and resources on earth into ever smaller pieces to support increasingly more people. Rather, the pie actually gets bigger with the addition of each person. Every individual human being actually bakes his or her own piece of that incredible pie! Even better, whereas people are born with a body and intellect that sustains them, that ability is not fixed. It can be enhanced, refined, and specialized to cause you to become ever-more differentiated and productive. We have what we are born with, and we also have everything that we invest in ourselves or others invest in us throughout our lives. We get better over time; the result of which is that we eventually produce more than we need. That excess allows us to prepare for the possibility of being less productive later in life and yet still maintain our standard of living. Is this a great system, or what? Well, it doesn't feel like that all the time.

The Econosphere's Tough Love

Consider some of the topical economic issues of our time, and how you might or might not view these issues depending on your understanding of the Econosphere and from where value really flows. Take for instance, the fear of trade. At its core, there's nothing alarming about trade, right? Someone somewhere makes something and is willing to trade it for something else made by someone living elsewhere. It sounds kind of nice in a sort of trade-bread-not-gunfire sort of way, doesn't it?

Oh, but how we worry about it. It makes some of us ache with fear; it makes others head to the street with signs and even bricks to throw through windows in protest. How can this simple exchange of talent and time generate such extreme passions? Why would you want to restrict the ability to trade the product of one person's toil for the product of another person's toil, and why does it matter if these exchanges take place over some distance?

The problem is that you do not live in the abstract. Exchanges of good and services, if you do not understand your economy as a system preserving sustainability and prosperity, might look something akin to anarchy, and within that anarchy there is one person in one land providing a good that could otherwise be produced domestically. Free trade can look a lot like theft: They're stealing our jobs! However, if you can see that if one region of the world can concentrate on those things that they do most efficiently, then another region can concentrate on what they do best. The end result is more goods for all because everyone would operate as efficiently as possible.

Part of the problem comes from the fact that we do not think as a region, or as a people. We are individuals; we think as individuals and, understandably, we value continuity and predictability in our lives. We are happiness maximizers within the Econosphere, and the happiness that we maximize is our own. If one person builds his life and his household around a particular vocation, community, or culture that is in turn built around a particular industry that is adversely affected by shifting comparative advantages around the globe, then talk of optimal efficiency is of no comfort at all! Free trade, certainly in the short term, has the potential to be upsetting, no question about it.

To see the industry where your parents toiled success-fully now fail and whither or to watch the town where you grew up crumble is a genuine loss that is hard to get over. So what is the answer? To some, it might seem that the solution is to control trade flows to protect industries and ways of life that might well disappear if forced to compete with every distant competitor. Protection always sounds comforting to some, particularly those directly and severely affected by the changes that do take place in the economy over time.

What Happens When We Try to Stop Change? Here's Your (1952) Buick!

Imagine if you could stop the forces of innovation by preserving every industry that we have today; every region might remain unchanged, and every person might never have to face the stress of moving, retraining, or scrapping previous expectations for life with new plans requiring the pursuit of a different field or even moving a household far away from the familiar. Now think of a place that has tried to isolate its Econosphere from the rest of the world, like North Korea or Cuba. Want to trade your car for a bicycle, or a 1952 Buick?

When you try to cut off all or part of your Econosphere from the real, global Econosphere, it's a little like trying to keep a rainstorm from sweeping across your state. Not only will you still get wet, but you're likely to catch a cold, too.

Trying to drop out of the Econosphere slows productivity, and living standards start to go down. We would no longer see advances in technology, medicines, or the phenomenally efficient services, like UPS and cell phones that we take for granted. You could afford fewer things than you otherwise could, and you would invest less than you otherwise would. You would create less than you otherwise create, understand less than you otherwise understand, and you would become less than you otherwise are.

Over the last few centuries, we have learned a lesson about our relationship with the biosphere. We have seen that attempting to impose mankind's will over nature often creates unintended negative consequences that make us all worse off, rather than better off. For instance, we have seen that the thoughtless damming of rivers can endanger fish and other wildlife, compromise the fertility of our land, or increase the risks that can come from extreme weather. We have learned that it is better to work in harmony with nature rather than to inflict our will wantonly upon it. We know that to ignore the contours of our physical world leads to flood, famine, disease, and illness.

Slowly but surely, the "green" movement has made us aware of our individual impact on the biosphere and put pressure on public and corporate policy to better align and harmonize with its protection. Whereas most people would not want the ascendancy of humans to somehow be impinged upon, we have become more intelligent about managing the impact on the biosphere because we see that it is in our best interest to respect what sustains us and that we cannot or should not control. We have even come to understand that our environment can provide some goods and services better than we can, whether that is natural topography shaped by centuries of forces or wild ecosystems that provide us with, say, food in the case of our oceans and rivers, or with a balance of plant and wildlife that maintain balance and livable space, so we correctly leave it up to nature.

You need to come to the same understanding when it comes to the Econosphere. The Econosphere is best left to encourage people to produce those goods that they have an advantage producing, as that production leads to maximum happiness. For those who have less comparative advantage in a particular area, the Econosphere encourages them to find other outputs for their talent. Although that might be harsh in the short term, and it often is, you cannot forget that you have two basic roles in the Econosphere: You create—and you consume—the work of others. Let's take a look at how these two sides of your life in the Econosphere interact.

The Protection Racket

Any tariff or barrier to trade that is erected to shelter an industry that can't compete is actually a subsidy for that producer and a tax on the consumer. Protect a T-shirt maker in Tennessee (and all the other American T-shirt makers) from those cheap T-shirt makers in Indonesia, and suddenly every T-shirt in America is going to cost more.

Same for cars and toasters and telephone answerers. So protecting one person, a business owner, or employee, by restricting the natural functioning of the Econosphere, takes away from every person who needs to buy that protected product because the price is going to go up.

But it gets worse. The impulse to try and fiddle with the incentives in the Econosphere (and go against its natural laws) causes the Econosphere to run less efficiently. Before long, with less competition, we get less output per worker, less per set of raw materials, and less per unit of time. On net, we all lose. Within that accounting, it is the consumer that gives up something to make the producer's life easier and less prone to change or stress. But who is looking out for the consumer? What did the consumer do to warrant having to bear such a cost? And let's not forget: We are all producers *and* consumers. Even the subsidized producer faces higher prices in the end result!

Over time, there are few one-for-one tradeoffs because lost efficiency in one area of the Econosphere hurts the entire ecosystem. Moreover, because we each put our individual finite energy into the Econosphere, the output that springs forth from the economy depends on us. We are not taking wealth from each other; all of us are the fountain from which the value springs. It might look as if some of us get wealthy on the backs of others sometimes, but the underlying truth is often obscured by the passions of the moment.

Feel like it's time for another law? You're right!

> ## The Fourth Law of the Econosphere
>
> **The Law of Plenty:**
> The Econosphere never takes from one to give to another.

The Kinder, Gentler Econosphere

The Econosphere is a natural system that challenges us to improve via competition, but it never takes away from our great shared wealth. What appears to be seizure are just shifting relative surpluses and deficits that affect market prices and incentives. This is another important point. In the Econosphere, for one to win, it does not dictate that another loses. It is a natural system that challenges us to improve via competition, but it never takes away in the aggregate.

It is clear that some people who do not fully grasp this natural system that sustains us might, in fact, believe that the untamed, wild Econosphere is a malevolent force robbing the weak or innocent. I believe that they are wrong. I would even go so far as to argue that the Econosphere is not even a neutral system. Rather, our economy is a benevolent system that rewards those who come to terms with it and learn to understand and live in harmony with it. I might also argue that the economy is forgiving in that it rarely takes away from those who otherwise are not believers and who see only anarchy in the workings of the Econosphere.

After all, you don't have to believe in the wisdom of the market to be governed by the economy's system of incentive and disincentives. It governs us all, and while it is a trusted advisor and mentor to those who see Adam Smith's "invisible hand" (where in a free market, an individual pursuing his own self-interest tends to also promote the good of his community as a whole) as a guide, others do not see a hand, but rather a cruel and random unseen force.

Even if personal outcomes from one person to another are at times similar, the personal experience and interpretation can be quite different. Remember, we are all utility maximizers, and we equate utility with happiness. Seeing the Econosphere for what it is and what it provides is certainly happier and more comforting than fearing perceived chaos. Without understanding the functioning of the economy, you might see only the outcomes without ever understanding the reason behind those outcomes, and that's just not any good at all.

2

Where Does the Economy Come From?

Where the economy comes from is a question that is almost never asked, and I guarantee you that if it were posed, say, on Sunday mornings on the various political policy TV shows, we would come away with many a YouTube-worthy answer! "The economy comes from natural resources." "The economy comes from good policy making." "The economy comes from the middle class." "The economy comes from me, and if you vote for me, I will...!" Well, now that I think of it, and as silly as it might sound, that last answer is about the closest to the truth as are any of the above answers.

Here's what you should do to think about the answer to this question. Start with the whole economy, and then start subtracting things until the economy no longer exists. And there you will find the source of the economy. Let's give it a try. Let's subtract, say, fancy pet shop gold fish from the economy. Okay, we still have an economy. Now, we'll subtract ground paprika. The economy is still there. How about we get rid of boats? ...still there. The Internet? ...still there. Oil? ...still there. Sure, we now have a world where we have animal-drawn carts, we can't cross oceans, our food is not particularly flavorful, and we don't have inhabitants for our fish bowls, but the economy is still there.

Let's break it all the way down to just five people and the federal government; that's still an economy. Now, subtract out the government; we still have five people bartering with one another. So does the economy come from people bartering with one another? Well, let's get rid of four people. Now you have one person, and that person spends his or her days collecting food and firewood, making clothing, working on shelter, and so on. All these things are products and services, all of which have differing relative value to our sole decision maker, and all of which are created or consumed based on individual preference. So, you know what? It's still an economy, albeit a particularly lonely subsistence economy (kind of like Tom Hanks on that island during *Castaway*, but without the volleyball).

Okay, now let's subtract our last person. Well, the food is still there, but there's no one to collect it. There's no need for shelter; there are no garments. In fact, there is no value because there is no demand. So now, there is no economy. Thus, it would seem that all you need is a single person, just one single person using his time and ability to produce and consume whatever is needed. It is the individual who is the sole fountain from which the economy springs forth. So, to that end, for the politician who credits herself as being the arbiter of our economic well-being, it might be said that she is correct in the sense that just as with anyone, the economy does indeed spill forth from within her. The economy comes from consumption of the human potential, both in the production of needed goods and services and in the enjoyment of time at leisure—and that even includes the activities of politicians who appear on Sunday morning political shows!

Now, I know what you are thinking: Fine, economic output comes out of each of us, but I'm not an example in a textbook and I am not Tom Hanks on a desert island; I am a real person, and I need a job! The economy that I care about starts with my earning a paycheck!

What Is a Job, Anyway?

Many of us work at a job, and it might be the case that as far as you are concerned, *your* economy comes from *your* job, and that's what is important! That is perfectly understandable. Still, if that job ever disappears, the basic understanding of where jobs come from will be important to you indeed.

So, what is a job, and how did it get there? How was it created, and why do some persist and others disappear? Well, first off a job actually isn't the key ingredient to economic bliss that it is made out to be; it is more or less an accounting device used to describe an exchange. The essence of a job is the exchange of one person's time or talent for the product of another's time and talent. It is the person who is working the job that is the key ingredient; the job is just a catchall description of the actions and the intentions of the person performing the task and the individual or firm who has retained that person to perform tasks.

Most of us work in exchange for currency; we don't barter directly. But that's just a matter of convenience. We aren't truly working for slips of paper, coins, or, in these days, electronic transfers of money into our bank accounts; we work for what those checks, bills, and coins can be traded for—the products of other people's work. As to the "job," in the most common application of the term, if a firm (a concept that we also do not tend to think about in a particularly thoughtful way; but we will a little later in Chapter 5, "The Firm as a Coalition") finds that it frequently needs the same kinds of output day-in-day-out, it will likely be convenient for that firm to put someone on retainer who can produce that output so that the firm does not have to start every day trying to contract anew for someone to perform the required task.

So, a firm creates an opening, generally with a concise description of what tasks will be performed, what skills or training are required, and what compensation will be returned in exchange for the completion of said tasks. The firm then goes about the process of finding and hiring a person who is willing and able to perform those tasks, and if a deal is to be struck, that person must agree to use his or her time and ability in the production of that good or service all the while keeping in mind the personal costs that will be incurred in the process and the value that will be derived from those goods and services eventually purchased with the compensation awarded. Geez, that's a long description for something as simple as a job—I guess that's why we came up with a concise name for it!

As long as the value of the compensation is of equal or greater value as the costs to the individual in performing these tasks—the costs can be measured as the value of whatever else the person would be doing if not at that job, and some allowance measuring exactly how unpleasant the job may be, as people demand higher relative compensation for a job they hate than a job they love—and as long as another set of tasks does not emerge that provides a better cost/benefit outcome, we have a deal, or in its most common usage, we have a "job!" And, over time, the firm itself will go through the same type of thinking on its end. As long as it is getting what it believes to be a favorable cost/benefit outcome, it will preserve that job in its present form and location and will seek to retain the person performing that work. On the other hand, if the opportunity to make a better deal emerges, the firm will likely take the opportunity to subsequently change the tasks incumbent in the job, change the person performing the job, or both.

And, even though it is the individual who brings much of the value produced in any job, we have set up our society so that having a formal job is extremely convenient and often times optimal. A job typically allows for some long-term planning on the part of the individual and more stability than if each day started with a search for opportunities to trade. Also, a job allows you to concentrate on what you do best, leaving the other tasks inherent in producing a full range of products to other workers who are also specializing in what they do best. If you tried to produce all the things that you consume, you would have far less to consume at the end of the day than you currently have. And, if you tried to produce every aspect of the products that your employer or firm produces, your firm would likely produce far less than it does. It is optimal to specialize in what you are most skilled at, which is another important part of why so many of us have jobs—the job allows us to be as productive as possible, and thus optimally compensated. But a job is not everything!

All Work and No Play Does Not Maximize Utility

Let's not forget we are utility maximizers; we are not fulfilled by working as much as humanly possible. In fact, we are fulfilled by working as little as possible while still producing enough tradable goods and services so that we can procure a reasonable amount of what we desire. At some point, your scarce leisure time is more valuable than the additional item that you can purchase through an additional hour of work, and it is at this point that we stop trading our valuable time for the production of goods and services. It is within us all to make that judgment, which we are always innately doing, and that's why our lives end up as some mixture of work and leisure. We each have our own unique mix of what we do to pay the bills and what we do so that we enjoy our lives.

The Econosphere Is Merely and Mundanely the Sum of Its Parts

Such is life; or, I should say, such is life for the individual. But what of the whole? The intention in this chapter is to discuss where the economy comes from. Instead, thus far, we have mostly discussed individuals and jobs; but there is a reason for that.

Do you know how people like to use the phrase "more than the sum of its parts" to describe things—particularly things that they really like. They might say, the 2008 Florida Rays team was more than the sum of its parts or, the Park Slope neighborhood in Brooklyn is more than the sum of its parts. It's nice to think of something as transcendent of its basic building blocks. For instance, I love Patsy's pizza (a Manhattan staple), particularly with olives and peppers on top, and I would like to think that it is somehow more than just flour, tomatoes, cheese, and such. Well, I also like the Econosphere because it provides me with everything that I need. It is elegant, seemingly fragile, but clearly resilient as seen through the lens of time. It encourages you to produce those things that are scarce and those things that are held in high regard by your fellow inhabitants, and it dissuades you from producing those goods and services that are already plentiful or not of value. But with all that said, although the 2008 Tampa Rays might have played beyond what its payroll suggested was possible, and although Patsy's pizza transcends its ingredients, I can tell you with great certainty that the economy, for all its beauty and complexity, is simply the sum of its parts.

It is your production, plus my production, plus your neighbors' production plus my neighbors' production, and so on. Add it all up, and that is the economy! When the economy is prosperous, we all produce goods and services of rising quality and quantity at an accelerating pace—

interestingly, it is not enough to just retain equal quality and a constant pace of production, as we tend to exhibit rising productivity over time, which is why wealth has risen over time. It is the nature of the Econosphere to reward innovation, a key element of rising worker productivity. Correspondingly, when the economy becomes unbalanced and falls into recession, our aggregate rate of productivity is slowed or has stalled.

It all hinges on how productive we are. We are the essential source of output. This point is often lost along the way. Certainly, there are many factors that affect our productivity. Do you live in a place that encourages the exchange of time and talent for the production of other people's talent—that is, do you have a free market in which to trade? Is there an infrastructure that allows transportation of people, information, and intermediate and finished goods? Are there enough educational resources so that you can enhance your abilities to produce more valuable goods and services, or produce a higher output of goods and services?

These essential factors needed to create aggregate wealth are particularly important at times when we consider public policy to improve our economic outcomes. Public policy, if and when it is applied to matters of the economy, should be focused on making us more productive. Too often, we focus on just about everything but these important things! This is more true in some countries than others, and more so in some eras than in others. Take for instance two of the great economic stories of recent decades: China and India.

Remember When China and India Were Polluting Their Econosphere?

In recent decades, China and India have enjoyed explosive increases in the wealth of their expansive and populous countries after many preceding decades of trying to impose their own economic systems of incentives, blocking the natural system of incentives provided by the Econosphere. These nations suffered terrible poverty during their failed experiments with collectivism—communism in China and socialism in India. It was only when their policies changed and began to let their people live in harmony within the Econosphere that these nations began to live up to their great potential (although it will take decades for the legacy poverty resulting from their previous, failed economic systems to be fully expunged).

Assuming these countries continue along this journey, their size combined with their still large deficit with the rest of the world as measured by worker productivity means that they can remain leaders in growth for many decades to come—they're still so far behind that their potential for improvement is almost unlimited. Both of these populous countries' histories are stunning examples of what negative repercussions can occur from attempting to eliminate market forces and erase the rules of the Econosphere. Moreover, these countries' rapid assents when market forces were invited back in are an equally impressive example of how rapid improvement can be achieved by simply choosing to live in harmony with our social environment, allowing prices to guide production, and entrusting each of us with the ability to make decisions based on our own unique talents and preferences.

In the examples of China and India, please note that there was no change in these nations' endowments or mix of natural resources. There was no sudden discovery of oil or gold. The only thing that changed was that the individual was empowered to guide his or her own economic contributions. In large part, the judgment of a select few was substituted with the billions of micro decisions that would otherwise occur quite naturally. And it is typically the case that billions of small decisions, which tend to be made with much more intimate, local knowledge and are made within a framework of personal relationships, tend to be much more informed and far less indiscriminate than relatively few, large, autocratic decisions; that is, thou shalt plant corn this year! Such centralized edicts were emblematic of China in decades past, lending to frequent over-supply for some commodities and severe shortages in others.

They Don't Make Big Heavy Chandeliers Like They Used To

Let me share a story about this notion of central planning versus pure market-driven activity that I was taught in school growing up. I have absolutely no idea if it is true, but I have no reason to believe that it is not and I would, at least, like to believe that a few of the things we are taught in school have their roots in actual events. More important though, it is a vivid example of how the best-intentioned central planning can lead to a perverse outcome.

Supposedly, in Russia during the Soviet era, a factory was commissioned to produce chandeliers. Now, in a market-driven system living in harmony with the overall Econosphere, a factory producing chandeliers would seek out potential buyers to better understand what sorts of chandeliers are desired and what prices the market can bear. The factory would endeavor to create the optimal mix of chandeliers and produce them as efficiently as possible to maximize the returns for the owners of the factory. In the case of our Soviet-era chandelier factory, the workers in the factory were, as are we all, utility maximizers, and set out to maximize their returns—they can tinker with our economic and political systems, but we are hardwired to maximize utility; no state can change that. There were no market prices to influence their output. Rather, the central planners decided to pay the factory bonuses based on the weight of its output. It was thought that would be a fair measurement of the overall productivity of the factory.

Thus, our clever utility-maximizing chandelier makers saw their incentive and set to work in meeting their objectives. They produced massively heavy chandeliers that in all practicality could not be hung from any normal ceiling, and for which there was no demand whatsoever. The maximum rewards came from producing the heaviest output possible, and that's just what they did. The factory produced giant, useless, ill-conceived chandeliers. In this case, individuals chose to maximize their utility by reacting to the incentives in front of them, and it was central planners who provided the wrong incentives.

As opposed to living in harmony within the Econosphere, the central planner tries to remove market-based pricing and create a new system of incentives. This is roughly equivalent to deciding that instead of placing a house in the proper location, taking into account local topography, you should flatten the hills, fill in the lakes and impose your own ideas of where water should run and where the land should rise and fall. As is the case in both the development of land and in the stewardship of an economy, there can be disastrous consequences to imposing your own will on what is otherwise an interdependent system of which you likely do not have a full understanding, thus increasing the likelihood of negatively affecting many other variables within the system and individuals who are not present to articulate their own preferences.

No matter what the powers that be might attempt to do *for* us, or more accurately, do *to* us, we are still going to try to maximize our happiness. We are born with a potential life span, which we can employ with whatever judgment and physical ability to any task at hand. We can also augment our abilities with education, training, and experience that can make us increasingly more valuable in the production of goods and services. We desire to make our own situations optimal, fulfilling tasks in the maintenance of our households, creating goods and services to trade for the products of others' toil, and all the while retaining as much leisure time as possible.

Our limited time drives us to be as productive as we can be as we work, so we can get the maximum reward for our toil and thus the maximum time to enjoy activities that are nonmarket-related, such as time with family and friends. The incentives encourage us to strive to make the best use of our time, our resources, and each other. It is a very slick and ingenious system.

Within that description, is there one core ingredient that makes it all possible? Is it desire or judgment? Is it education or ability? Well, it is all those things, but those things emanate from one basic commodity: the individual. We are the essential raw material! Without people, everything else is worthless. And it is the sum of all our activities that makes up the whole of the economy. The economy comes from us!

Each morning triggers in us that basic desire to better ourselves by producing goods and services that will be valued by our fellow man. We trade among ourselves the best we can so that we support ourselves and our families and still retain as much leisure time to enjoy our personal pursuits and the company of others. It is beautiful choreography indeed, performed on a global scale and evident everywhere one might look.

In fact, as I type these words this morning, I am watching the sun come up over Hong Kong from my hotel window. The harbor, once still and reflective of the moonlight has now absolutely come to life with boats of every size and configuration zipping to and fro. Nature is providing us sun, warmth, water, and so on...and people are springing forth to create value with this day that they are given.

3

A Lifetime of Opportunities

Life in the Econosphere might sound a bit antiseptic, given the stark terms in which it is described, I realize. All these inborn inclinations to maximize utility and issues of inadequate information and insipient interference to the natural ways of things might seem a bit, well, unnatural. I suppose it is different from the usual analysis of how the world works. Yet, you can be assured that all the unique and wonderful things that you run into through the course of your life do, in fact, fit into this framework.

The Econosphere does not necessarily inform you what exactly to do; rather it informs the decision making that gets you where you want to go. This explains the immense variety of output and ideas that make this world such an interesting place in which to live. There is no perfect outcome shared by all, other than the desire for maximum happiness (or utility). That can lead you to climb a mountain, work as a computer programmer, have ten kids, go to school, sleep late, or become a monk, but everything that leads to these decisions are economic decisions, and they happen in accordance with the rules of the Econosphere.

Does this seem farfetched? Well, let's take a look at a typical life (or two), and try to understand what sorts of decisions and incentives guide us along. More important, we will try to see how these decisions are inevitably guided by the rules of the Econosphere. Those rules apply to a mid-level office manager and parent of two trying to find a home to purchase, the same way it applies to an awkward teenager trying to find a date for the dance. As different as those experiences can be, at their core, they are more or less the same.

1964: Bundles of Economic Potential and Joy

So, let's start at the beginning. I hereby announce the blessed arrival of baby Milton Tiberius Dickens and baby Charlotte Margaret Rand. Each a cherished blessing to their families I can assure you! There's no telling what baby Milt and baby Charlotte might accomplish in their lives after all! Imagine the things that they will see!

Well, we surely cannot imagine all the details and wonders that they will experience, but we certainly do understand the timeless rules of the Econosphere within which they will operate, and as such, we can imagine the types of decisions and incentives they will undoubtedly face. In fact, it might be instructive to our exercise of understanding the functioning of the Econosphere and to better grasp our own opportunities to think a bit about what lies ahead for Milt and Charlotte. We might see ourselves and our own families in their adventures and accomplishments. And wouldn't you know; Milt and Charlotte actually live just

down the street from one another, which will make it easier
to keep an eye on the both of them!

Place: The Product of Generations of Economic Incentives

Milt and Charlotte both live in the Fox Run housing
development right off from Plank Bridge Road in Pickleboro. Forgive the odd name of the town. You see, some of
the state's largest cucumber farms were located right here
not more than about fifty or sixty years ago. They used to
ship pickles all around the country. The cucumber farms
and the pickling facilities are long gone now. (Well, in the
here and now, one of the pickle factories is a brew pub,
cleverly named "Pickled Pub," that also serves pizza baked
in an old-fashioned wood-fired oven and has bowls of
homemade pickles right on the table, but it's no longer a
pickle factory.) People around here think it is a shame that
the industry is gone; it's one of those industries where hard-
working immigrants from Europe worked hard, raised families, and built this country! And now it's all gone; what a
shame! Where are those kinds of jobs today?

Truthfully, the cucumbers were here because the
immigrants that settled in this area early in the 19th century
were good produce farmers and came in search of fertile
and affordable land. It just so happened that they also
brought along with them a traditional knowledge of the
canning and pickling processes that were gained from generations of storing produce over the winter. It was a bit by
accident that pickles became a primary export from this

area; after people began growing produce here, and because the country's economic system embraced entrepreneurship, loans could be procured, far-away markets accessed, and businesses built from little more than hard work and determination. Upward mobility was hampered by neither social caste nor restrictive laws here in the United States, at least not for these European immigrants, and as such, a pickle industry was built!

The industry was successful to the extent that the local children, perhaps for the first time in these families' histories, were afforded a good secondary education. This produced doctors, engineers, architects, scientists, teachers, and lawyers among other vocations. Generations of children fanned out around the country with no limits to either their own mobility or potential, with only their own utility maximization in mind. Many ended up in Bigton, a city about fifteen miles away that was growing quickly at the time. It was growing quickly enough that the city soon spread into the surrounding farm land.

This increased the value of the land in Pickleboro and other nearby towns, enriching the farmers as they retired and sold their land. But this also changed Pickleboro and many neighboring farm communities into commuter towns. Not a bad thing, of course, but some of this development took place oddly fast, ill-thought-out perhaps, and spread eerily and unnaturally wide. Considering federal and state initiatives that led to vast road development and implicit subsidization of the growing car culture and the industrial complex that supported it, and also the increased subsidization of homeownership through lending programs, this type of development, with hindsight, could have been expected.

Heck, if government is going to explicitly make it worth our while to shift to a bedroom community model with bigger houses and lots and slightly longer commutes via private auto as the only initial downside, we as a nation will choose to take advantage of it. Remember, we are all utility maximizers, and a large part of the information with which we can make decisions comes from market prices. All things held equal, if one good or service is made less expensive than a competing or substitute good, either naturally or due to policy, we will choose the less expensive item.

But back to the suburbanization of Pickleboro, with more kids seeking their fortunes in the cities, and with greater ease of transportation making more fertile land accessible in the South and West, there wasn't much reason for the cucumber industry to stay put. Land prices in the area were rising with the building of new communities, as were real estate taxes, so it was a logical time to cash out.

It is said that time heals all wounds. Skipping forward a decade or so, during the last half of the 20th century, the town that Milt and Charlotte were born into eventually transcended its role as the somewhat uninspiring bedroom community that had its genesis in misguided policy, pushing families off to the edges of metropolitan areas. Since then, things have filled in a bit, a more industrially diverse local economy has formed, and the majority of people do not even commute downtown any longer—they mostly commute in and around the other suburban communities within the greater metropolitan economy. So things have gotten a bit more pleasant, particularly as the government incentives that had initially created some of these far-off suburbs have lost their value as land prices were bid up and the time cost of commuting increased exponentially. Incentives are now a bit more natural, for lack of a better word.

The Occupation of Infants? Being Cute and Cuddly

So, back to Milt and Charlotte and their lives in Fox Run right off Plank Bridge Road in Pickleboro—at the present, our heroes are just babies, and as such, their options are a bit narrow. Lack of language skills, limited mobility, and little knowledge of basic hygiene protocol all leave Milt and Charlotte with few career or lifestyle choices. They're essentially stuck where they are, and their immediate local economy is just what they have within their own households.

For the time being, there are few products or services that they can produce and with which they can trade. Their basic needs are straightforward enough; food, shelter, and diaper services are the basics. Beyond this, there is a desire for interesting toys with which to occupy themselves, and utilize to build more advanced and tradable skills. Finally, there is also a basic emotional attachment that Milt and Charlotte will seek out throughout their lives, as we are social creatures at our core—building relationships is per-haps our most important skill allowing us to specialize and trade for what we need throughout our lives. Thus, an inclination to create a social network has become encoded in us through the generations. And for now, that's about everything that Milt and Charlotte are involved with.

It seems like a pretty basic list of needs. Moreover, they barely take up any room given their small size and lack of assets. That said, their list of what they can produce to procure their needs is perhaps even more limited. In some ways, given the lack of skills yet acquired, this is one of the more daunting times to get by in the Econosphere. Milt and Charlotte essentially have two things with which they can trade. First off, they are cute and they have come to realize this as an asset. Gooing and gawing, cuddling, smiling for pictures, and such...clearly elicits favorable behavior toward them. The more they play the part, the more attention they receive and the better the quality of care that they can acquire. At this age, cute pays the bills; so, it's show time.

There is, of course, another darker way to get what they want, as well—let's call it their nuclear option. Although not to be deployed at all times, Milt and Charlotte have found that they can bribe people into providing for them with negative behavior—or more precisely, the promise to cease negative behavior. Screaming and kicking can be used to procure items quickly, not because there is a demand for screaming and kicking, but rather a demand for that behavior to stop. It is a bit of a mob-style tactic, but the bad behavior creates what is known as a negative externality. It essentially exacts a cost from those affected by it.

In the adult world, there are usually laws that protect people from negative externalities. For instance, there is zoning that seeks to protect landowners from undesirable activities taking place on adjacent lots, there are noise restrictions, restrictions on public smoking, restrictions on telemarketers, laws against bribery, and so on. I'm not saying that these laws are the best way to handle such issues, but they do exist.

Fortunately for Milt and Charlotte, there are no laws against bad behavior on the part of babies within their homes or in the grocery store. As such, there is no protection for the other members of the household. These household members are incented to find ways to make the bad behavior stop, which often requires payment of some kind of bribe. Milt and Charlotte have found that with limits they can get what they want by creating a negative externality.

This is essentially the classic two-product economic system. You might be more familiar with the example of a guns and butter economy, where a simple two-product economy maximizes its collective utility by producing some mixture of those two outputs. The same is the case with Milt and Charlotte. Some mixture of being cute and being bad procures them the highest value basket of goods and services, and thus their incentive is to find that optimal mix—smile for the camera during the holidays, scream your lungs out in the checkout line at the grocery store, and get what you want when you want it! That's utility maximization at its most primal level!

That's the life of a baby; things get more complicated thereafter, but in some ways they also become more straightforward.

1970: A Little Bit Older, A Little Bit Wiser

Let's skip a few years ahead; Milt and Charlotte are both attending Pickle Meadows Elementary School, and things have changed a bit for them. They have acquired new skills allowing for greater mobility and communication, but they still remain dependent on their families for food, shelter, and transportation beyond a short radius. They also have a new product: a report card. Aside from being intermittently cute and bad, their production is now monitored and scored at school.

Interestingly, communities have created a pseudo market system in which children produce output, mostly in the form of reading and writing assignments and mathematical calculations, which they subsequently trade for what they hope will be a high value. However, the interesting twist is that the immediate rewards are not consumable goods or currency. Rather, output is traded for letter grades (A through F usually, skipping E for some odd reason). These letter grades are then returned home, and their quality largely dictates one's treatment within the family. A's are rewarded, perhaps with gifts or increased freedoms. F's are punished with restrictions such as fewer entertainment options or less mobility. Even worse, a string of F's generates punishment at school, including a complete disassociation from one's social network of peers by either changes in one's assigned classes or the complete removal from one's age group.

In some ways it is almost more interesting to wonder about the motivations of creating such a system than to ponder the activities and motivations within the system. Certainly communities have long-run incentives to continue to improve their functioning as a marketplace in which goods and services can be traded. The higher the quality of human capital that communities produce within their schools, the higher-valued will be its goods and services.

As to parents, the incentives are a bit more obtuse. Schools provide training for their children and baby-sitting services, allowing parents to perform work aside from child rearing. Moreover, training provided in schools should allow the family unit to perform collectively at a higher level. Education also provides the possibility of children eventually becoming independent, and also eventually providing services to the parent in later years. Finally, one can fathom that a tendency to help one's offspring to succeed leads to successful children, which in turn carry that same tendency as these children raise the next generation.

Regardless, Milt and Charlotte are stuck in school, for better or worse. A few generations ago, they might have been picking cucumbers most of the day. Today, however, they spend much of their day learning to be literate and civil. They have long since differentiated between a dog and a cat. They know that cows live on farms. They're roughly familiar with U.S. history involving the Pilgrims and George Washington. They're also dipping their toes into mathematics by adding and subtracting small numbers. Their most basic motivation is to master these topics and return home with papers, assignments, and report cards adorned with letter grades of A's and B's. If successful, these grades can be exchanged for ice cream, increased television time, video games, and more. It's a refreshingly simple system, if only the other details of school life were as simple.

Of Cooties and Other Social Bugaboos

There are also the increasingly complex social interactions between Charlotte, Milt, and their peers. At this point, despite the proximity in which they live and their similarity in age, interaction between Milt and Charlotte is limited. Recently, Milt has identified cooties on Charlotte. This has prompted Milt to steer clear of his cootie-afflicted peer, except of course to remind Charlotte intermittently of her cootie affliction. Charlotte, on the other hand, feels this diagnosis to be in error, and wishes nothing to do with the source of the erroneous accusations.

Truthfully, much of the interaction between Charlotte and Milt has nothing to do with their relationship, but rather the relationships with their respective peers. Both Milt and Charlotte are beginning to form social networks with which they will trade goods and services. For now, those services might be little more than recreational activities, access to backyard pools, and entrance into the best birth-day parties, but the actual act of aligning oneself according to one's own self-interests is roughly the same as what Milt and Charlotte will be doing throughout their lives as utility maximizers.

In the case of Milt, this has broken down mostly into athletic feats on the playground, picking on girls such as Charlotte, and acts of defiance to school rules. In the case of Charlotte, she too is an athlete having mastered both the double-dutch jump rope technique and hopscotch. More-over, aside from this, her social interaction is a bit more nuanced than Milt's thus far, because it encompasses popu-lar tastes in fashion and music, and interestingly enough, she is scoring points with friends for her indifference toward Milt and his cootie taunts.

Truthfully, throughout their schooling years, the rituals will change, but the basic forces driving behavior will remain the same. They will basically break down into two categories: scholastic and social. The measurement of scholastic merit will remain the same throughout most of Milt's and Charlotte's educations. The grades will denote achievement; achievement will produce preferred results. Over time, these preferred results will change in nature. In Pickle Meadows Elementary, it might entirely encompass treats from one's parents. Later on though, good grades will be rewarded with entrance into desired, higher-achieving classes, and in the end, higher grades will grant entrance into a wider array of universities or influence employers to grant Milt or Charlotte a job of his or her choice or a higher starting salary. By which time, Milt and Charlotte will be familiar in the process of producing work in return for a reward, and also in the understanding that better performance produces better rewards.

The social interactions and judgments do mature over time however, chiefly as the desired outcomes change. And, I suppose we would be foolish to skip over these. After all, people are utility maximizers, and as we stated before, utility is roughly analogous to happiness. The work and reward system that prevails describes a case where output is created in exchange for currency. This is partially analogous to happiness because money can be exchanged for just about anything. Thus, if there is something out there that can be purchased and will make you happy, then the possession of currency with which to procure such items should make you happier. Notwithstanding, money is not a perfect proxy for happiness; I believe it was the Beatles who pointed out rather deftly that "money can't by me love."

To dive into this topic and otherwise advance the story of Milt and Charlotte, we should move on to their shared college years—they both proudly entered State U. after graduation. Much happened at this time, and we must first touch upon Milt's and Charlotte's changed relationship, as they both left high school as sweethearts, which influenced their decision to attend school together.

1980: Charlotte and Milton Sitting in a Tree, K-I-S-S-I-N-G

You see, despite Milt's previous assertions of Charlotte's cootie infestation, with time, not only did Charlotte forget about Milt's youthful taunting, Milt too amended his thinking on the subject. Instead, Charlotte's and Milt's familiarity with each other having grown up in close proximity, combined with a number of shared friendships created a bond between the two teens. This, combined with their mutual rising interest in romantic relations, sealed the deal. They became an item.

Now, as we are talking about the Econosphere and the forces within, we must note that their decision to date was based on individual desires to maximize individual utility. Part of this is biological in that they were physically attracted to one another, and as an economist, I have no desire to go into the biological processes that, among other things, allow us to perpetuate our species. Let's just leave it that the desires incumbent in this process are inborn and are one of the many factors that prompt us to choose a mate, or at least a boyfriend or girlfriend.

Beyond the biology and related emotions, however, there are still the usual incentives that have driven these two, and all of us, since birth. In this case, the products that Milt and Charlotte have to trade between each other are those things that come with their companionship. These things might be the act of frequently listening to the other's ideas and concerns, participation in shared interests or the interests of the other, sexual favors, the extension of social status from the other, the receiving of gifts or experiences such as meals or entertainment, and off on the horizon for these two, the possibility of eventually creating a prospering household.

Enhancing the romantic attraction between the two, Milt had become a varsity athlete with a scholarship to State U. He also worked a few days after school and on weekends and subsequently had money to spend and a car with which to provide mobility for the pair. Charlotte was a star in her own right in that she was active in student government, was a good student, and a member of a socially active clique of friends. She shared an interest in school sports with Milt and was also college bound. They each brought status, activities, and shared interests with which they freely traded between each other so that each of their individual utility was maximized as a result of their shared relationship. So much so that they headed off to college together. A match made in heaven, right?

1982: Milt, Why Weren't You in Class This Morning?

Well, maybe, but one year later, Milt's interests have changed a bit now that he has hit college, or perhaps the pair's differences have become more evident in the new environment. The problems have a great deal to do with the differing discount rates that Milt and Charlotte apply to their future potential gains—a discount rate is essentially the rate at which someone discounts future utility relative to utility today. Would you rather have one dollar today, or two dollars tomorrow? If you apply a large discount rate on a dollar tomorrow, the answer might be that you want that single dollar today. If you apply a small discount rate, you would want to hold out for those two dollars tomorrow. A more familiar and relevant question to our story may be, do you want to study tonight to increase the chances of landing a good job four years from now, or would you rather go to the kegger in the woods behind Alumni Hall?

Charlotte applies a much smaller discount rate on her future. It is important for her to not only gain the skills she will need for a good career, but she is also interested in networking and associating herself with those who will help her to succeed in the years ahead. Milt, on the other hand, misses the job he had in high school and the money it afforded him, he is interested in his collegiate athletic career, but he is also interested in the active social life that college offers—two interests that are for the most part, unfortunately, mutually exclusive.

Thus, we have a dilemma. Milt, based on the information in front of him and the high discount he applies to future success, finds himself a happy-go-lucky partier, who also rides the bench at his games and is supporting a C-average, 20 extra pounds, and a pretty good hangover most days. But, he is maximizing his utility based on his own unique set of preferences and the information he has at hand. At the least, he's having a really good time.

Charlotte, on the other hand, is up early, doing well, active in organizations, and has avoided the added beer-weight.

Her new friends don't like Milt, and Milt thinks her friends are nerds. This relationship is on the road to ruin; and mind you, it is not because Milt is wrong or that Charlotte is right. Rather, their mutual interests have dissolved, and their utility is maximized by keeping the company of others outside of their fragile union. In fact, what was one of the premier relationships in their high school ended with a whimper, as Milt simply opted not to return to State U. after his freshman year and went back to work full-time. In sum, Milt likes money in his pocket and the freedom to spend it; Charlotte is forgoing short-term gratification by preparing for a future she hopes to acquire.

1998: Charlotte the Yuppie and Milt the Townie

And wouldn't you know, Charlotte is as good as her word. At thirty-four, she finds herself living with a former colleague, Bernard, who began as an associate with her on an investment team at Bigton's biggest investment bank. They have since each received advanced degrees and a good deal of success in their careers. A rented brownstone in Bigton, a luxury sedan, significant investment holdings, and upper-class friends with whom they share interest in many fine things; whether it be food, wine, travel, art, and such. Charlotte, the girl who once was ostracized due to her cooties, is now a coveted attendee on the benefit circuit! Clearly, she is a utility maximizer who had better information than had her old beau Milt.

Poor old Milt is, in fact, still stuck in Pickleboro. He doesn't live far from the old Fox Run development in which he and Charlotte grew up. Poor guy; he was once a big man on campus, and now he's just a townie. Since he left college, he went back to work with the same contractor he had worked for during high school. Over the years though, he has acquired new skills and experience and about ten years ago, he went out on his own. Helped by a resurgence in investment in residential and commercial real estate, he has stayed busy.

He's up early to work every day, but he's also home pretty early, and his life in his hometown does afford him the opportunity to maintain friendships with many of the people with whom he grew up, as well as remain close with his family who are all still local. Speaking of social life, apparently there are women in Pickleboro who appreciate the company of a guy who has his own business, his own house, and a big truck. To date, he's never been one to settle down, but he hasn't been lonely. On most weekends, he's usually out at Pickled Pub with friends, family, and whomever he might be dating at the time.

Milt is a utility maximizer, just the same as Charlotte. It didn't lead him where it led her, but that doesn't mean that his utility would be higher if he was with Charlotte in Bigton. They each have their own preferences, their own unique skills, and their own set of information, which is always imperfect, but we do the best that we can with what we have.

Imperfect information, in fact, is the chief factor that keeps us from maximizing our utility at any one time. You go to where you think you will find the greatest success and happiness, given all the information that you have, but on occasion, when you get there, you find that your treasure map was either incomplete or just plain wrong.

Speaking of which, Charlotte's and Bernie's life has taken some interesting twists of late, as both Charlotte and Bernie have moved their careers more into the high-tech arena. Bernie has been involved largely with the IPO and M&A processes involving high-tech startups and he has taken significant positions in many of these firms. Charlotte has moved into the PR arena, geared toward the positioning and marketing of new Internet commerce firms. Charlotte and Bernie hope to enter the 21st century with financial independence!

There are a few downsides, however. Charlotte and Bernie don't see each other all that often. Each works late, and each travels frequently. Of late, it has occurred to Charlotte that she had expected to be married with a few kids by now, and hopefully striking a balance between home and work, sharing the load with a doting Bernie. Time gets away from you, however, particularly when the rewards of concentrating one's time and effort elsewhere are so high.

2000: Tech-Wreck in Bigton; Renovation Boom in Pickleboro

Another issue on Charlotte's mind is that Bernie has changed a bit of late. He's downright irritable at times and less accessible than he used to be, either out late at night or traveling seemingly for the sake of traveling. Charlotte knows he's just working hard; yet one tangible thing that has changed rather noticeably is that he is less forthcoming about his end of the financial picture. Charlotte is paid mostly through salary, whereas Bernie is paid mostly in stock and a year-end bonus based on the fees that he generates for the firm. Bernie is also mostly in charge of Charlotte's and his investments, many of which are speculative and to date quite leveraged. He's doing a great job, so Charlotte believes. They've been doing great thus far anyway, with significant unrealized capital gains.

Back in Pickleboro and moving forward in time a bit, Milt still can't believe that it's the 21st century! He's just excited that the lights still turn on and that the worst predictions of mass systems failure didn't happen; he's not going to need that home generator he bought, though he can probably use it at work and recoup the cost. That said, his stereo doesn't work anymore, and he suspects the 2000 bug has something to do with it; it had a digital tuner after all. Regardless, life moves along.

These last several months, the newspaper at the end of Milt's driveway each day has been focusing on the tech-wreck. Milt's a bit mesmerized. A few of his clients have been affected, but to tell you the truth, to Milt, falling stock prices on the Nasdaq feels a world away from Pickleboro. Low interest rates and enthusiasm for housing as an investment has kept things moving along for him! Let the fancy people in Bigton worry about their Internet stocks!

Little does Milt realize that one of those fancy people, his old friend Charlotte, has lost her job. Looking around, she can't understand how she could find herself in this situation. She had planned everything so carefully. But that's not the worst of it. Bernie and the finances he controlled have taken a serious turn for the worse. His job is gone, as are their investments. Bernie is clearly in shock and clearly not handling these losses in stride. He blames Charlotte; he claims he would be happy in a life as a carefree bachelor in the Caribbean by now if it weren't for his having to support Charlotte over all these years. He drinks, he smells, he's not the man she thought he was.

They can't pay the rent on the townhouse. Their savings and income are gone. They can't even make the car payment. Had their information been better, had stocks always appreciated as they had believed, had the high-tech niches that they both pursued proven less volatile, they would be fine. Had their expected income stream been more conservative, they would not have found themselves so overextended. Had they not concentrated so much on their careers, perhaps their relationship would have matured enough to better allow them to be of more support to each other now that they face their first taste of adversity.

It is too late for what-ifs now. Too much has been lost; and too little is shared between them. Bernie heads out west to become a ski bum. Charlotte slinks back home to live with her parents. Neither expects to ever rekindle their careers.

Compounding things, life at Charlotte's parent's home is as humiliating as she feared. All that work and nothing to show for it, that is except for several new wrinkles on her face and a handful of outstanding loan balances. The skills and attributes that she is in possession of are no longer worth as much in the marketplace as they once were. Her utility has waned; she has little confidence that she has good information on how to succeed going forward. That said, she is and always will be a utility maximizer, and each day, she naturally takes what information is available to her along with the skills and aptitude that she has, and applies it in such a way that she makes the best of her situation.

2002: Home Again

One day, this process led her to offer to take out the garbage for her father as a show of gratitude for his hospitality. Wouldn't you know that Milt happened to be driving by on his way to visit his folks down the street just as Charlotte was lugging out the garbage can. Milt, of course, took the opportunity to stop and get a few jabs in at Charlotte, because he does believe that Charlotte treated him a bit shabbily in the waning days of their prior relationship. That said, Milt is a content person and figures that he is likely to derive more pleasure from rekindling an old friendship than exacting some comeuppance. And he chooses to invite Charlotte to Pickled Pub this Friday to dine with him and his friends and family.

Mind you, Milt and Charlotte left one another when their utility was no longer maximized by being together. Charlotte's path to higher utility, she believed, was best derived by study and networking. Milt, on the other hand, derived his highest utility from partying and eventually heading home to work. Times change though, and although Milt appears to have the upper hand now, he also finds himself without a consistent partner with which to share experiences, and both he and Charlotte are conscious of their growing desire to start a family.

It's Not Just Candy and Flowers; There Is Math Involved

Now this sounds all quaint and nice, fit for a movie on the Hallmark channel, but there are exacting calculations taking place subconsciously behind the scenes that make this a little more than just candy and flowers. For instance, Charlotte's high pay in years past meant that her time at work was far more valuable than her calculation of the utility that she would receive by working less and procreating. Now, however, with the crumbling of her industry, her time at work is worth far less, thus tipping the scales so that the relative utility derived by breeding outweighs her other current choices.

As for Milt, the marginal costs of taking on a wife and child are relatively small. His housing costs are fixed, and there is plenty of room for a family in his home with little additional expense. By his calculation, his income will not be interrupted with the addition of a wife and child, and the cost of the additional mouth to feed may well be offset by Milt's savings by not hanging out at Pickled Pub most nights of the week. The math has turned in favor of Charlotte and Milt rekindling their relationship; and as you might expect given what we know of the ways of the Econosphere and utility maximization, wedding bells soon follow!

A happy ending? Well, it is hard to say. What we do know is that Milt and Charlotte will continue to be utility maximizers. Their lives will continue to be a mix of work time and leisure time. Moreover, they will always utilize the information that they have to make decisions about the direction of their lives, and we do know that the quality of their outcomes will be mostly reliant on their individual skills and the quality of their information.

For our purposes here, I don't think we need to go through this couples' ongoing years in great detail. But I will share with you this; Milt and Charlotte do stay together and raise a nice family. There are ups and downs; similar to the ups and downs that they have already faced. For instance, Charlotte's years at the investment bank and as a PR executive were not as worthless as she believed in 2001. As they grew their family, Charlotte took on a partnership role in Milt's business, greatly improving its financial situation and expanding the company's marketshare so that it grew to have several crews out working for the firm simultaneously. Moreover, when Charlotte got Milt's business in order, she hung out her own shingle and helped other peoples' businesses for a nice fee, and this time, she was careful to not be too dependent on just one industry as she was prior to the high-tech bust.

Moreover, Charlotte paid Milt back for his kindness in the wake of the tech bust when their business was badly bruised during the housing bust several years later. Her additional income and the empathy that came along with their relationship's maturity made the experience much less painful than it otherwise would have been for Milt.

Even Bernie eventually got himself together. After decompressing and becoming a bit more emotionally well-rounded after a few stress-free years of being a ski instructor, Bernie's investment banking career was rekindled in the economic recovery, and although his chosen industry would face additional volatility in the subsequent recession, he was better protected the next time around as his hard-earned experience caused him to make better decisions by not becoming so over-leveraged and undiversified. This time around, his information was greatly improved.

Milt, Charlotte, Bernie, you, and I make decisions everyday, many of which have nothing to do with career, money, or investments. Yet they are all still economic decisions. The economy springs forth from our own life span. As such, any decision relating to the consumption of one's life is an economic decision. To smile for the camera or to throw a fit in the grocery store; to study or party; to marry or remain single; to be an investment banker or a ski bum; to order a salad or a pizza; these are all economic decisions made according to the Econosphere's rules with the information at hand and always to maximize utility. It is just that simple. Should you find a new job, move to a new city, or have a baby? That depends on your preferences, the associated costs and benefits, your skills and abilities, and the information that you have in front of you. The first two variables are largely fixed; the latter two items can be improved upon. And that is where the individual can concentrate to improve one's outcome.

We are always trying to better ourselves and our situation. Oftentimes that might mean keeping up with our peers, which is, conveniently, the next topic on our agenda.

4

Why's My Piece of the Pie Smaller Than His? The Gift of Inequality

In the Econosphere, inequality is the source of our discontent—also our ambition.

Now we get to the meat of it. We must dive into the source of our great discontent. Why is it that the Smiths have it all? They're paid more. They have more stuff. Their house is larger, their car is better, their fingers are forever pruney from the long hours spent in their saltwater lap pool (and they don't even swim laps in it; the lazy bums just float around at one end!). Surely, an injustice has been perpetrated upon us.

Give us back our share! There has been a terrible wrong! The Smiths don't deserve it, I can tell you that much. That's our lap pool, not theirs.

It sounds petty, almost ridiculous, to make this argument. Each of us is out there every day witnessing inequality to such an extent that we have largely come to terms with much of it. But we will likely never be at peace with it. And that might be a good thing, considering that it is inequality—the possibility of putting in effort and bettering yourself without having to carry everyone else along on your back—that is the primary fuel of the Econosphere.

Depending on the circumstance, we can chalk it up to greater risk taking or higher intelligence, dumb luck, or access to better education. The Smiths might have simply inherited their ample and lush piles of lucre. The lucky dogs! However, all of us see inequality, and we likely put a judgment value on who deserves wealth and who does not.

For instance, folks, if I can generalize, tend to like people who create tangible, useful goods and services, and do not begrudge the sources of these innovations their money. You might conclude that Ray Kroc or Steve Jobs deserve(d) everything they earn(ed)—and, of course, if you have made it this far into the book, you may be feeling the same way. But how do you feel about CEO pay in general? How about the pay of politicians or lawyers? What do you think about inherited wealth? Do you see Steve Jobs and Paris Hilton as equally deserving of their respective fortunes?

First, deserve is a value-loaded term, so let's drop that immediately. You might have your favorite glitterati among the so-called "beautiful people" and your not so favorite, but we can nonetheless point to respective sources of wealth and say, "Here's why, and here is where it came from" and if it was generated within the rules of society (that is, not against the law), then it is no one's right to say who deserves what. Rather, we should step back and see where wealth—or more broadly, utility—comes from, and then, use that knowledge to maximize utility for ourselves. This is, after all, the thrust of our philosophy. We must learn to see more clearly and appreciate the functioning of our economy, and subsequently use this heightened sensitivity of the economy's incentives to better direct our own actions, leading us to become more productive and better rewarded for our efforts.

Through this chapter, we explore the origins of wealth and our incentives to acquire it. We examine why some people seemingly fail or fall behind in the acquisition of wealth and why others might succeed. We also look at the function of the state in both perpetuating and minimizing inequality across the economy, and we note the necessary underlying framework of a plausible state effort to minimize inequality—if the state were to deem this a desirable goal. Most of all, throughout the chapter, I want to reinforce the notion that one person's wealth does not necessarily come at the expense of another. One person can earn six figures per year, while another might bring home five, but the raw materials that make this possible are not shared and distributed among us, but rather are unique to us and have much of their base in each individual human life span and the inborn abilities that are within each of us.

We're All Utility Maximizers; Just Some Are Better at It Than Others

Wealth is what we tend to point to as an apparent measure of success, but that isn't what we as humans aim to maximize. Humans are utility maximizers. Utility is a somewhat opaque economics term, but we can think of it as another term for happiness or pleasure. We each want to maximize our happiness. For some, that might be lying on a beach

and eating beans and rice, for another that can mean helping others in need, and for still others, it can mean man-
sions, lobster, and a yacht. All are perfectly fine. Money is a
pretty good proxy for utility, but that is only because it can
be traded for many necessary and desirable goods and services. Stored money can even provide us years on the beach
if we want to go that route at some point in time. Money is
a store of value and is an accounting of the worth of accrued
labor. It's the value of what we produce and trade with the
rest of our fellow humans. As such, money often does provide a convenient measure of the utility that we derive.
Most human's lives are based around trading with others,
and money is the medium that makes this process quick
and convenient.

As to your own utility, the good news is that you're
already working to maximize it. Utility maximization is just
like breathing. You're born with it.

And, of course, the bad news is that you have only a
finite number of people to blame that you don't have more
to show for your time and energy. The real determiner of
the marginal improvement or decay in your situation is
only you—you can't even blame CEOs, lawyers, or Paris
Hilton.

It's Not a Zero-Sum Game

Inequality is actually a good thing. For those who have
not stopped to ponder our economic incentives, this premise can be a bit of a kick in the teeth, but it's necessary to get

it out there. Folks who see the world as a competition only—a zero-sum game (an interaction in which one participant's gains result only from another's equivalent losses)—will point out that there have to be winners and losers. The notion that our economy distills down to a zero-sum, winner-take-all competition is entirely untrue. There is plenty of room for winners and more winners. If you look around, for instance, you see mostly winners. Okay, some cynics might see only losers, but I see winners.

Think about the things that keep you up at night. What if I lose my job? What if I can't afford my mortgage? Who would want me? How can I compete with those hungry kids coming out of school? How can I compete with people who have more experience? How can I compete against people with more money and a more prestigious education? There's only one job and 10,000 applicants!

This is the kind of anxiety that, in my experience, can absolutely possess you. It's not all bad, mind you, because it focuses you a bit more to apply yourself, but for folks who ruin their health and happiness worrying about such things, I might suggest a little travel. Actually, you don't even have to leave the area you live in. Just take a drive around or better yet, take a walk in a city and look up at the office buildings. What you see are thousands of lit office windows; on the street level there are thousands of retail establishments operating and surrounding those are thousands of occupied residential units. Each and every day, billions of workers are at some task somewhere, returning home each night, most to their own home or apartment, where their household, whatever its shape or size, exists without starvation or eviction.

This is the story of the vast majority of people out there. Who says there is no such thing as a win-win scenario! Yes, there are homeless and poor. In major downtowns, there are beggars on every corner. But the vast majority of folks are out there doing what they do, and getting by! And regarding many of these panhandlers, I pass many of the same urban corners each day, and I am often amazed at their longevity. I'm not saying that there are not better ways for them to spend their time, but I have to hand it to them on their dedication to their vocation of panhandling—some are far better at getting to the "job" on time than many other supposedly upstanding citizens I know.

Back to all those occupied places of business. What do people do in all those offices? Where does the money come from? The answer to what these folks are doing is almost irrelevant. Who cares what they are doing? Understand only that they are trading their leisure time for productive time, generating income with which they will purchase the equivalent value of goods, services, and savings in return. All these folks are out there attempting to be as productive as possible while maximizing their own utility. All are motivated within their own realm of knowledge, using the information at their disposal and deciding on how much of their leisure time should be spent in market activity to maximize their happiness. That is what's going on out there.

So, in this context, where does the zero-sum notion come in? When we try to balance the equation, or slice the "pie" into pieces, how does your win diminish the size of the piece of pie for someone else? Surely, there must be a variable in an equation somewhere in some textbook that says that an additional unit of income to Mr. and Mrs. Smith means one less dollar that can go to everyone else. And guess what? If it exists, that textbook is not worth the paper it is printed on.

As discussed in Chapter 2, "Where Does the Economy Come From?" the Econosphere's size is not fixed. Theoretically, its potential size might be fixed at any one particular time, but we're never anywhere near its potential, at least as far as I can imagine. We're capable of so much more, as evidenced in part by our long-increasing productivity and wealth—we don't seem to be anywhere near a point of diminishing marginal returns. Moreover, our nagging information problem, that problem when we don't know everything that we need to know to make precisely the right decisions and direct our energy to the most productive tasks, is far from being solved. Imperfect information is the primary source of our not realizing our maximum potential aggregate output. I know at least a dozen people who have exceedingly bad information problems, and in my estimation, are operating at less than their potential— hopefully they don't read this, because I haven't had the heart to give them my assessment. Regardless, my main point is that the economy is not a fixed-sized pie to be divided up.

As to the information problem, a large part of many peoples' information woes is that they do not understand or even see the Econosphere in which they toil and cannot fathom how they create value in the marketplace or direct themselves to maximize utility. Although knowledge of the Econosphere cannot precisely foretell when a company's books might be cooked or whether one house is a better purchase than another, it does allow an individual a framework with which to evaluate what information is available to make the best possible assessment of the options at hand.

What Are the Sources of Dissimilar Wealth?

Think in terms of the individual when imagining aggregate output or wealth or happiness or whatever the overarching metric that you prefer. The size of the Econosphere is based on individual decisions that are made, as alluded to in previous chapters, at the most micro of levels.

Just because your neighbor is sitting in that lap pool, it doesn't have a thing to do with the absence of your own lap pool. In fact, the Smiths could have a lap pool, a Jacuzzi, and a steam shower—perhaps even an outdoor convection oven—it would be absolutely no skin off your back! Wish them well, and figure out a way to be more productive.

Moreover, there is nothing that says that Mr. and Mrs. Smith are any happier than the person who sells them their newspaper in the morning, or even the guy on the corner who asks for Mr. Smith's spare change every morning. There are only individual decisions, made with the available information and according to unique preferences and ability. Be happy for the Smiths, and quit scowling at them over the fence; they might actually invite you over for a barbeque some time if you're nice.

I suppose that just making nice to the Smiths will not entirely sooth your anxiety stemming from their good fortune, however. So let's take a closer look at how the Smiths might have done it. What we'll discover is that there are not that many disparate ways that one can gain wealth.

How to Consider Inherited Wealth

I think the most contentious of the ways that one can become wealthy is by just being born. Nothing ticks-off people more so than when someone else gets a head start on amassing wealth. It's not fair, right? Well, although I might be jealous of such folks, I still can't quite point and say that anything is particularly unfair about being born into money.

After all, what is inherited wealth? Inherited wealth is nothing but stored labor from a previous generation. Grandpa Larry worked all his life, spent frugally, invested smartly, and died with a nice nest egg. And maybe you were lucky enough to be bequeathed a piece of it. What is the matter with that? Why would anyone begrudge you a piece of Grandpa Larry's hard work? As it turns out, Grandpa Larry traded more leisure for work than he apparently needed to. So, he didn't live long enough to spend it. Silly Larry. Maybe he should have spent more time at the beach!

Still, Larry might not have been all that silly. After all, Larry didn't know how long he was going to live, so maybe he erred on the side of caution. He probably slept better while he was alive because of the nest egg that he built up. There could also be another reason why he worked too much, saved too much, and didn't stop to smell the roses more often; he just might have wanted to hand something down to you, the apple of his eye.

You inherited some of Larry's leftover labor. And, believe it or not, it is a matter of public policy that there is something wrong with that. The existence of gift and estate taxes are explicitly because the state wants to take some of Larry's leftover labor to redistribute it to other people—people who Larry didn't even know or maybe even like! The intellectual justification for the inheritance tax is that income earned and amassed over life must have come at the expense of someone else—a notion that flies in the face of what I would consider basic economic theory and certainly contradicts the basic edicts of this book.

Interestingly, the state's tradition of taxing dividends, interest, and capital gains actually creates an incentive for those amassing wealth to become less productive as they become more wealthy—there is already a diminishing return (a concept that we explore shortly) from each additional dollar saved, but taxing savings and investments at a high rate only compounds this natural effect. As to Larry, he must not have gotten the message that the nest egg he was working to leave behind would be viewed with such derision and held up as something ill-gotten on the part of his benefactors; he could have spent his golden years consuming more and producing less had he known. Of course,

Larry lying on the beach, as opposed to toiling at work, decreases society's overall aggregated wealth, but who am I to question the wise men and women who formulate tax policy?

But what truly gets people when it comes to peers that get their money the old-fashioned way, by inheriting it, is that they are given an unfair head start! This is, in my mind, one of the most interesting claims about the apparent negative affects of inherited wealth.

I can share with you one thing from my book of experiences (and we'll follow with the theoretical explanation thereafter), there is no better way to make a kid less productive than by giving him or her money. I've known a fair number of people who have inherited considerable money, and a good number of folks who have not. Let me tell you, there's a difference. Anyone can be a screw-up! But to be a truly special and notable screw-up, it takes money!

You might conclude that I have found myself amid an unusually dim-witted group of heirs and heiresses. However, my experience is not unusual; it's just a basic rule of economics. It's called the law of diminishing marginal returns. That is to say that each additional dollar brings less additional happiness than the one that preceded it. As such, a person is willing to trade fewer additional hours of leisure for each additional dollar than the one that preceded it.

For folks who already have lots of dollars (that is, many possessions and significant savings and investments), chances are that they will be willing to trade less leisure for productive time working in the marketplace than the person who has far fewer dollars in the bank. Thus, if we can return to the notion of the rich kid with the unfair advantage, although that kid may be having a ball, he is likely to put less effort into market activity than he puts into the annual snowboarding trip in Tibet or into becoming a better tennis player. These kids are happy, but their inherited wealth might just end up making them less of a producer of marginal wealth than they would have been otherwise.

People shouldn't fear rich kids. Feel free to envy them if you want, but do note that their lucky circumstance has put them at a significant disadvantage when competing against someone with a relatively smaller stash of cash and thus a greater incentive to work hard and succeed. When you consider who you might be out there in the world competing with, you should plan on raising your game to hold your own with the talented and hungry kids!

Earned Wealth

No one should worry, per se, about the talented and hungry. They should, however, be prepared to witness these people make the most gains in terms of their productivity. As such, they are likely to make the most progress in terms of wage and salary growth. And there are good reasons for this.

First, note that I am prefacing "hungry" with "talented." Talent is of great value in the marketplace. After all, no one needs to be terribly competitive with or jealous of the inept and hungry. In fact, the former condition is likely to be a contributing factor to the latter.

Talent here suggests abilities that are appreciated by others, and this appreciation is what allows a person to trade time-producing goods and services that are valued to the extent that other market participants are willing to trade a tangible amount of their own labor and stored labor in exchange for that output. The greater the talent, we assume, the higher valued is the output.

In a simplistic example, LeBron James has earned far more money (other people's stored labor) playing basketball than I have. This is a result of his talent, which in turn allows him to trade time playing basketball for an inordinate amount of other peoples' stored labor. Meanwhile, I have made absolutely no money playing basketball, because no one is willing to trade their own time and abilities to watch me play. It's sad but true. I'm forced to play for free, with only my own enjoyment as a reward—basketball has to be leisure time for me; while it is productive time in the marketplace for Mr. James.

If you couple the ability to produce highly valued goods and services with the hungry moniker, it suggests that marginal returns are near their maximum for each additional unit of leisure time traded. You should also note that hungry is as important a variable in this exchange as is talent. A talented person, having already amassed considerable wealth, might well choose to, say, retire early or switch to an occupation that is more enjoyable, but less monetarily rewarding. For instance, how many bed and breakfasts are actually the highest market use of the innkeepers' time and abilities? Same with tearooms, antique stores, and art galleries. The world is a far, far better place for having all these things, I just always wonder whether many of them would exist if the proprietors were motivated by a concern about where their next meal would come from.

Talent and hunger are key determinants to whatever you might harvest from working and trading in the marketplace. They are the will and the way to wealth. Ironically, folks who are talented and hungry are not likely to be on the radar screens of those worried about inequality, due to the hungry part. After they have traded enough of their talent to be noticeably wealthy, they are likely to be somewhere on the way to moving from hungry to stuffed. Going back to our neighbors, the Smiths, they're not hungry, and thus, they may no longer be in possession of the drive that got them where they are. Nonetheless, it still might drive you nuts to watch them float around in that pool all day.

Those Either Not So Hungry or Not So Talented

So what about the rest of us who are not among the extremely talented and hungry? That's just the way that it goes? There are the rich, the ambitious and talented, and then the rest of us? I suppose there is a reason why our news is full of celebrities and the incredibly wealthy. At the very least, the rest of us want to know what it's like to be them.

Does the possibility of becoming like them drive others to strive to improve their own lot in life? Yes, the cults of imitation that surround these folks seem to make that case. The free-market economy is all about striving for that brass ring, and assuming that striving improves our ability and skill in providing goods or services to the market economy for which participants are willing to trade significant labor of their own is what creates wealth to begin with. Now, it might not be the case that kids imitating LeBron James, Justin Timberlake, or even Steve Jobs are actually leading to real gains in wealth. In fact, in some cases, you might conclude that it has worked against them; but that's not an indictment on the system. Rather, it is illustrative of an information problem—the free-trading marketplace of goods, services, and ideas is nearly flawless; unfortunately, the quality of our information is highly imperfect, affecting our ability to be as productive as we might be.

Perfect Market, Imperfect Information

In the Econosphere, not everyone becomes fabulously rich, even if they want it really, really badly and work day and night to achieve it. That might be the case for a few reasons.

The first problem is typically an information problem. The information bugaboo is at the core of both micro economic problems, such as bankruptcies and personal distress, and also major macro economic events, such as recessions and market crashes. You see, markets are perfect, but information is imperfect.

If the kid who wants to be LeBron James knew that he will never come close to reaching that goal, and that the time and effort put into that task along with the opportunity costs of not pursuing other opportunities would all go unrewarded, unless that kid derived a tremendous amount of utility from being a poor, obscure playground basketball player, he would never pursue that goal. If an investor knew that the stock she just purchased was about to decline, the purchase would never be made. If a widget manufacturer knew that the bottom was going to fall out of the widget market, it would have never produced so many unsold widgets.

We, as utility maximizers, always have the best of intentions in mind, and we are always attempting to maximize our happiness and well-being, but sometimes we do the wrong things because we have poor information. Heck, people jump off of bridges because they think that their utility maximizing option is to no longer exist. Either they were right, or they had a serious information problem!

That problem, the information problem, has unilaterally undone many a dream to achieve some goal. For now, it is just a fact of life. I would argue that information is getting better all the time, particularly with the advancement of information technology, modern database practices, and statistical techniques. Moreover, because through trade and exchange we are increasingly bringing the world together as a single marketplace, there is more and better information to be harvested and used for self-betterment and profit. So, in a real sense, our rising productivity is, in part, thanks to efforts to solve the information problem. Is it solved? Well, considering the market volatility still evident every day, I would say that we're not even close!

Aside from the information problem, what else might keep an individual from Warren Buffet status? A big part of it might be that it's just not in the individual. I have never met a person who was not gifted in some way. But individual gifts are not equally valued in the marketplace, I'm sorry to say.

I went to high school with a guy who could juggle really, really well. We called him Jugglin' Jim. He could juggle just about anything: balls, hoops, bean bags, you name it. Sometimes, he would tell you to throw in something additional; whatever you had in your hand. So he would be juggling, say, beanbags, and he would say, "Throw Jugglin' Jim that calculator"—yes, Jugglin' Jim would refer to himself in the third person. So, you would throw it to him, and he would juggle the calculator along with the beanbags. What do you think of that? He eventually became a birthday party clown. As far as I know, he is the happiest guy around, and his utility is perfectly maximized by being a juggling birthday party clown. He clearly is acting, given the information and abilities at his disposal, to maximize his utility. However, he will not be lounging in his own saltwater lap pool like the Smiths, nor is he likely to amass inheritable riches, as did Grandpa Larry. He's just a juggling clown...and that pays about $400 per event, last I heard. He's a happy, juggling, moderate-income clown.

A clown, music shop worker, seamstress, waitress, draftsman, machine operator, accountant, train conductor, lawyer, movie star, or senator: Is there any real difference to the motivations and principals as to why people end up doing what they're doing? Not at all. At any given moment, each person is exercising the best possibility amid a limited selection of options open to that individual at any moment given imperfect information, available capital, and whatever abilities he has to better himself.

For some of us, that means juggling. For another, that could mean running a multibillion-dollar global corporation. There is no knock against either occupation. But don't expect each to be rewarded by the market equally. Depending on the circumstance, the market might value the output of one higher than the other.

Over time, however, there is greater opportunity to advance one's cause. At any given time, there might be only a handful of practical options to pursue in a given day. Across a month or a year, however, increasingly more options become variable. If Jugglin' Jim does want to change his lot in life, in a year's time, he might make a career change. In a few years' time, he can acquire training in a different field. In five years' time, people might stop calling him Jugglin' Jim; he might be just Jim, Mr. Talbot, or even "Sir."

Understanding where value is created in the Econosphere, and that acquiring wealth is a matter of trading your leisure time for time spent in the market producing goods and services and trading them for equally valued goods and services produced by others goes a long way in understanding that we are not in a zero-sum game. Identifying and developing highly valued skills and improving your information problem helps to improve your lot in the Econosphere.

What to Do About Inequality

Oh, but how we worry about that juggling clown! Around the time that I am writing this, the U.S. electorate just swept into office a whole gaggle of lawmakers who ran largely on the principle that it is government's job to correct the inequitable treatment suffered by my friend Jugglin' Jim. If that new gaggle of lawmakers reach their stated goal, we're going to take income away from the previously mentioned CEOs, lawyers, movie stars, and others who make higher than average income and give that money to Jim— or, I should say, we're going to take more money from the CEO and his ilk than we currently do and provide additional services and preferential treatment to folks in Jim's income bracket. The assumption being that somehow, the disparity between the relative awards garnered by the CEO and Jim represent a victimization, for lack of a better term. In this, we return to the concept of the zero-sum game where society, as maintained by government, is capable of producing only so much wealth. Thus, greater wealth for one means less wealth for another. Thus, we have a problem to solve. And that problem is chiefly solved through tax policy aimed at income redistribution.

Now, talk of income redistribution and things of that nature, sounds particularly pointed, biased, and provocative as it comes off the lips or appears on one's screen as one types. To those schooled in free-market economics, it is an ugly phrase. For those schooled in populist sentiment, it sounds about right, although the term "income redistribution" is often softened and hidden behind phraseology referring to the "squeezing of the middle class," "leveling the playing field," or "fairness." In fact, income redistribution is written into a good portion of the revenue gathering and fiscal expenditures of all levels of government. And it is typically supported by those who benefit from it, and tolerated by those who do not, because it is seen as a small price to pay for maintaining the status quo.

We get more specifically into various government policies in Chapter 6, "Stupid Policy Tricks," but in this chapter, as long as we are acknowledging income and wealth inequality and the role that it takes in our process of maximizing utility, we might at least look briefly as to the role that government might play either minimizing or perpetuating the inequality. It's funny to think that in many ways, it might actually be government's primary function to perpetuate income disparities. I suppose in a real way, the rule of law is all about perpetuating various levels of wealth. When I think about the rule of law, the first things I visualize are police cars cruising neighborhoods looking for those who might be involved in property crimes: burglarizing houses, stealing cars, and looting stores. Beyond that, I picture the police also in place largely to thwart violent crimes such as muggings, kidnapping, home invasions, and the like. I know the police do many more things than that, but I do tend to think of the police as mostly protecting citizens from other citizens who would like to forcibly reallocate wealth under the cover of darkness or at the end of a gun barrel.

Given that it would likely be a more productive endeavor to rob someone who has more stuff or money than does oneself, I suppose that robbery is a primal form of wealth redistribution. And because one of the primary services of government is the writing and enforcing of the rule of law, I would have to conclude that one of the primary functions of government is to perpetuate economic inequality. Jugglin' Jim might well end up in jail if he attempts to kidnap and ransom Grandpa Larry.

Thus, Jim kept on juggling and Grandpa Larry passed on his wealth to his heirs. In the same vein, you might just walk across the Smith's backyard and haul them out of that saltwater lap pool and declare it your own, but you likely choose not to, and if I am right about that, I would guess that Mr. Smith is either a lot bigger than you, owns a gun, or you have grown up with a healthy respect for the law.

In this sense, we must conclude that government does help the cause of the wealthy. Furthermore, our usually smoothly operating central banking apparatus and, thus far, its good track record in managing our currency is a benefit to all of us operating in the marketplace. We all benefit from the knowledge that we can trade labor for currency, and turn around and buy goods and services of equal value with that currency. That is a good thing. However, given the massive and well-paying occupations that have flourished within our increasingly complex financial markets, we also cannot help but wonder whether the beneficial fiscal situation created and maintained by our government does not benefit some more than others. Yes, Jugglin' Jim does benefit from his ability to trade juggling for cash, but those who speculate in the Treasury market might, on average, benefit more so than Jim. And those folks involved in arbitrage of Treasury options are also likely to be well educated in sophisticated financial techniques and, well, advanced education tends to be more available to those with wealth.

You probably can see where I'm going here. It would seem that not only do we have the police out there making sure that citizens are not reallocating wealth on their own at the end of a gun barrel, we are also creating a complex and dynamic economic system that seems more easily exploitable by those who have managed to acquire the skills and knowledge to understand these complex tasks.

In return, it has perhaps become economically expedient for those who have found success in acquiring wealth (the rich) to accept moderately punitive treatment in the tax code. It is oft argued that those who benefit most from our economic system should also pay more to maintain it. It's essentially fiscal tithing, with the IRS acting as a large, watchful, and insistent church usher in charge of passing the plate down the pews. It is tempting to leave it at that. A common phrase used around tax time by those who pay taxes is that there are no sure things except death and taxes. It's a bit of harmless gallows humor offered up by those who trade their leisure time for productive time in the market place, and then are compelled to relinquish a share of the gains derived from that process. Tax revenues are used to provide basic government services and fund some of the previously mentioned programs aimed at redistributing wealth. And that's okay with most people, but we should be careful to not be overly glib about the subject of taxes as an efficient method of decreasing income inequality.

First, to say that paying taxes is okay with everyone is a bit too easy. Yes, our tax code does do a pretty good job of keeping track of taxable income and vacuuming up that portion that is due to the government. However, to say that this process is not disrupting to the allocation of economic effort is to ignore the great effort made by many people to avoid paying taxes.

It comes in so many forms so frequently that you barely notice it any longer. It is the contractor who prefers to get paid in cash. It's the waiter or waitress who declares only a share of his or her tips. It's the side of business that never gets acknowledged on a person's tax return. And it is the leaps and mental contortions made in claiming question-able deductions. It's the wealthy household which, by virtue of their large savings, has financial advisors who are paid to devise methods to exploit the tax code. It is also the hedge fund manager, who by virtue of his financial support for the campaigns of elected officials, retains favorable treatment of the ways in which he compensates himself.

We're all friends here, so let's be perfectly honest. There is a multibillion-dollar industry built around tax preparation and advice. Money does not flow to this indus-try because it's nice to have a buddy help you with filling out the form! These folks, from the basic tax preparer to the accountant to the highest priced tax lawyer, can help their clients pay less in taxes than they otherwise would if they just went through the typical paces of filling out the form and sending in the check. It is an entire industry, creating wealth in its own right, mind you, dedicated entirely to directing activity away from participating in the government's income redistribution initiatives.

Now, this process is not as bad as it sounds. From the vantage of our discussion of economic incentives and how personal decisions play a vital role in acquiring wealth, the fact that we see a massive and effective effort in resisting the taking of acquired wealth is confirmation that individuals are active participants in their own financial processes. It is also a confirmation of the working of the Econosphere. Individuals in possession of a life span, natural abilities, and learned skills have the opportunity to trade their time in exchange for other peoples' skills and output. In this case, taxpayers need to find ways to retain more of their earnings, and there are those who are skilled or interested in researching how that can be done.

With the creation of a tax code, we find an entire industry born in its wake aiming to profit from its exploitation. There is nothing random about this. Participants who understand their incentives to trade time for reward or to keep more of their earnings find a way to trade, each skillfully maximizing his or her utility. Knowledge of the Econosphere makes you more efficient in exploiting this system—understanding how wealth is created and avoiding the anxiety and poor decision making that plagues those who cannot see the forest for the trees.

Now, as to the merits of this system that so many are artfully exploiting, there are many economists who make the argument that a large government sector is preferable, because average citizens are not fully deft enough to properly manage their financial and economic lives. That is to say, it is best for government to either directly allocate wealth or to create programs, such as the home mortgage tax deduction, 401k accounts, and the taxation of vices to better communicate to the masses what activities are socially preferable and personally responsible. For instance, just using the previously mentioned programs, public tax policy is explicitly rewarding those citizens who have borrowed money for the purchase of a home, are saving for their retirement, and who do not smoke or drink alcohol. Or you can turn that around and accurately describe said policies as punishing the taxpayer who is a renter, not saving for retirement, and enjoys drinking and smoking.

Such a description sounds novel, almost tongue-in-cheek, mostly because these programs are not marketed in the political arena as such. However, that does not make the preceding descriptions inaccurate. And, as mentioned previously, we do have a large wing of our economic thinkers advocating such policies. Moreover, wouldn't you know, these same economists are often gainfully employed in the creation and application of said policies. And no, if you were wondering, not all economists are involved in public policy; a good number of them are involved in the private sector helping to minimize risks and maximize returns for themselves and their employers—we are not all on the public dole.

But as to public policy, it is amusing to think that even socialist-leaning economists—economists who are skeptical of the market economy's capability to equitably distribute resources or correct imbalances and return itself to an optimal level of employment and output—act to maximize their own individual wealth, in this case by creating theories and programs that will in turn provide full employment for them and their colleagues! In this sense, their existence is almost refreshing in the context of the points that we make in this chapter. Despite the economic distortions and contorted incentives created by their policies, their actions confirm the basic premise of our thesis of wealth creation—even socialist economists act to maximize their own utility. Admittedly though, their actions do make it more difficult for the rest of us to create and accumulate our own wealth. In that sense, we can put them in the same box as the armed robbers skulking in the darkness previously mentioned in this chapter; they make themselves wealthier at the expense of their victims.

If Not Taxes, Then What?

In our discussion about income inequality, we should acknowledge that if the public sector does deem it to be something we as a society should hope to minimize, then let's at least advise how that might best be accomplished, other than just taking more money away from renters and smokers and implicitly giving it to homeowners and teetotalers.

Well, it's a pretty simple fact that policy does not create wealth, or happiness for that matter. People create wealth by giving up leisure time for productive time. At the extreme, if you have lots of government policy, but no people, there is no wealth creation. If you have lots of people and no government policy, you still will create wealth—we can argue whether there is more wealth or less in the absence of policy some other time.

If people are the key to creating wealth, what can government do to help the individual create wealth for himself? The individual takes what ability and information that he has along with physical and financial capital, which is less so at the discretion of the individual in many cases, and applies those things to be as productive as possible when trading leisure time for productive time. So, more or less, there's time and then there is the productivity. So, if policy is going to help the individual maximize utility, it either has to create more time or more productivity. Assuming we don't want the government mandating a minimum work-week for us all, we should look at productivity. Aside from the things that government already does, like provide the rule of law, roads on which to travel, and other niceties, policy might best be pointed toward increasing the ingredients of productivity: ability and information. Government could also provide financial and physical capital, but that would be an implicit redistribution of income and, perhaps more important, there is not necessarily anyone with the skill and prescience to decide who gets what and when. So it's best to steer clear of this hornet's nest entirely, allowing the billions of market participants to value competing uses for financial and physical capital.

Other than what we're born with, a good bit of the ability that we enter the workforce with comes from our formal education. Better education should allow us to employ an even larger quiver of useful abilities. The more skilled and knowledgeable you are, the more productive you will be. Moreover, the more skills, the more options one will have in selecting occupations with which to maximize utility. If Jugglin' Jim could both juggle and build houses, he might still choose to be a juggling clown, but if his priorities or views were to change, he could change jobs as well. Moreover, if cyclical demand for clowns turned downward, he could stay employed by pounding nails, and if demand for housing were to dry up, he could pick up the beanbags and red nose anew.

And then, there is information. Information is a valuable and powerful commodity, indeed. As for the United States, there is no economy in the world that has as much and as good public data on the economy, demographics, financial markets, and much more. Publicly available economic and financial data creates tremendous transparency for those who know how to apply it. But, how many people actually use it, or know how to use it? Greater tutoring as to what public information resources are available and how to decipher it would help businesses and individuals make better decisions. Moreover, while the United States has the best information available, that doesn't mean that it couldn't be better.

Any government policy that helps augment ability or improve information will, by definition, increase wealth, all other things held equal. And because such public services are offered for free and with revenue that is collected from income taxes, then such policy is a moderate wealth transference, paid for mostly by the rich and by corporations and used by everyone, and thus a mild force in decreasing income inequality. If increased in scope and quality, it would be a roundabout way to transfer productivity, as opposed to just stored labor, from the wealthy to the poor.

However, just try to run for office on a platform of increasing the amount of data made available through the Bureau of Economic Analysis or the Census Bureau! Good luck with that!

Barring Incremental Policy, What Can the Individual Do?

You can't hold your breath hoping for truly meaningful policy to decrease inequality to your benefit, particularly if you don't want these policies to end up decreasing aggregate wealth. Taking money from one person and giving it to another, which is the thrust of an income redistribution program, is good news for one, bad news for another, and decreases the incentive for either party to actually work.

Thus, income redistribution programs cause the aggregate wealth within the Econosphere to contract. That's not necessarily an immediate bad thing for the person on the receiving end of the wealth transfer. However, at the extreme, it has shown to eventually lead to fewer opportunities for individuals to trade their products and services for other useful products and services.

Moreover, you can't change government policy immediately, and unless you are a particularly persuasive agent for change, it would be a tough order regardless of the time frame. Also, let's get this notion about evicting the Smiths forcibly from their pool out of our heads. It's just not neighborly. Nor can you simply go out and get a Grandpa Larry who will be nice enough to die and give you money on the spot. So, let's not worry about that either. You might have a rich, older relative, but I doubt you're rooting for them to pass away so that you can cash in on her stored labor.

Actually, the only way to increase your wealth is to control the two things that you control every day: your productivity and the hours you work. You can spend more or less time working each day, and that is mostly dictated by the relative rewards of work and leisure. The question you ask yourself is, "Will I get more reward from working an additional hour or relaxing?" That's a decision you make every day without even knowing that you're doing it, so why start worrying about it now? You've got it covered.

Make the Econosphere Work for You!

Ultimately, your ability to make money or make more money comes down to productivity. That is the key to increasing your utility! The more productive you are, the more value your labor will hold when you trade it in the market for the output yielded from others' labor. Productivity, to the extent that it can be affected by the individual, relies on human capital (that is, ability and information). Essentially, human capital covers, "What can you do?" Information covers exactly what you should be doing, where, and for how much. The broader concept of productivity also covers things like the financial and physical capital available at the firm. You can do nothing to augment these things in the near term. However, better information tells you where these vital raw materials exist and allows you to decide to work at the firm that provides the best opportunity for high productivity and high rewards.

If you're really interested in getting a saltwater lap pool like the Smiths or if you're Jugglin' Jim and sick of the birthday party circuit, and you're thus far stymied in your efforts in getting ahead, there are two things you can do: Augment ability and improve information. Maybe greater information, for instance, will give Jugglin' Jim access to higher paying juggling jobs—corporate juggling team-building workshops, perhaps! As to ability, although I would guess that that is a bit more difficult to change in the near term, certainly greater information about what sorts of skills are needed in the Econosphere, and then the acquisition of those skills, is a prime way to increase wealth and utility.

Just don't count on this effort decreasing inequality. Nor should you want it to. Just because you are getting ahead, it doesn't necessarily come at the expense of someone else.

Inequality is the fuel in the economy's tank. The ability to get ahead without having to bring everyone else along with you is the basic engine of a free-market economy. It is the impetus of economic output itself. Moreover, today's inequality is simply the current outcome of generations of decisions about work and leisure. And, although there is little you can do about all the decisions that have been made before your own time, you can at least realize how the system works and start making the right decisions with regard to acquiring and deploying ability and productive effort. And, as mentioned at the beginning of this chapter, the good news is that you're already doing it. Now though, as you at least acknowledge that you are doing it yourself and why, you can apply a bit more thought to it and concentrate on doing a better job of it, and a large part of that is understanding how the Econosphere works and how to operate within it. If you get that part right, and your aim is to be like the Smith's, there is no reason to believe that that saltwater pool is beyond your grasp.

5

The Firm as a Coalition

Thus far, we have established that the economy emanates from each of us. The ultimate renewable resource is people. We are essentially trading portions of our own life span in exchange for others' products and services. We do this by portioning out our lives between time at leisure and time at work. During that time at work, we produce goods and services that we believe will be valuable to others so that we can trade them for the largest basket of goods and services that we can. The more productive we are, the less leisure time we might need to sacrifice to maintain or establish the quality of life that we desire. Our ultimate desire is to maximize our own utility, that is, happiness.

Moreover, as we do this, we add to the overall size of the Econosphere—we increase aggregate wealth. It is not simply an effort of getting your slice of the pie. You bake your own slice. Your success is not necessarily someone else's loss. If everyone succeeds, we are all better off. And the best way to help all of this along is to live in harmony with our social environment, the Econosphere.

We must allow the Econosphere to portion out resources to the highest uses and indicate relative surpluses and deficits via natural market pricing. In the same way that we have learned that we cannot force our will upon our natural physical landscape for fear of unintended consequences, we cannot force our will on our social environment. We must allow capital to flow just as we allow rivers to flow. We must allow the migration of physical resources and labor in the same way that we must allow animals to migrate. We should revere our social landscape, not mow it down as past generations did to our physical landscape when they tore down mountains and filled in valleys.

But although I hope these themes will resonate with all of us, and although the soaring themes can be inspiring, we must keep both feet grounded in the reality of our situation. Let's face it; when the alarm rings in the morning, you do not leap out of bed with the thought to create a basket of goods and services that you hope to trade with other people for all the things you need. There is no happy global open-air market where we all go with our basket of goodies to barter for our fondest desires—I'll trade you a poem and two handcrafted bowls for two roasted chickens and a Toyota Camry. No, when the alarm goes off, we're not off to find our special place in the universe; most of us are headed off to work!

Slave to the Corporate Machine

Work likely looks and sounds nothing like what we have described. There might be a desk, or a spot on the floor where you stand, and you do not dream of optimal output.

Rather, you have a piece of a task that you must complete for your employer to put together a whole line of products and services. You might be so far away from those final products that the ultimate output can seem completely removed from whatever it is that you do each day. You don't go off and trade your output with others. Instead, you likely get a check for the hours you put in, or a salary, or fees, or tips. And it is a grind. (There's a reason why they have to pay you just to show up, after all! If it were fun, you'd probably do it for free!) You show up, do what you were hired for, and then go home.

You eventually get paid and then you subsequently pay the mortgage or the electric bill or pay down your credit cards, and so on. So what does any of the soaring rhetoric in this book have to do with the reality of life? Where is this Econosphere? After all, most of us are just slaves to the corporate machine!

I suppose the "corporate machine" is an issue we need to discuss. Even when we step back to see that the money that we work for is simply a store of value allowing us to be more efficient in our exchange of goods and services with others, the role of the firm in this process still might seem like an unnatural presence. In a simpler world, each of us would trade a simple product, say, a basket of carrots or a cord of wood, for other simple products and services. Such a world would be a simpler one to understand; that's for sure. Still, if we were all vegetable farmers, firewood choppers, poets, basket weavers, fishmongers, and bakers, who among us would provide us with our cars, mutual funds, air transportation, pharmaceuticals, or fiber optics? Those things are more than a one-person job!

Thus, when a project calls for more than one mind, more than one strong back, significant physical assets, and ongoing access to investment capital, we naturally form a coalition, or by another term, a firm. As we try to understand what a firm is, it does not help that corporations have become one of the most demonized concepts in our popular culture. For the sake of better interpreting your own life within the Econosphere, try not to think of a firm as a permanent, faceless, hierarchical machine enriching the owners of capital at the expense of labor—I think that's a close representation of how the popular press and many policy makers describe large businesses. Rather, think of the firm more as a "happening," and not a perpetual entity. Particularly in today's service-oriented economy where much of our production is borne from human creativity as opposed to the extraction and movement of raw materials, firms function more as a serendipitous coalition of willing individuals, than as the cold, unchanging, uncaring institutions of our popular mythology.

A Firm Is Serendipity

Could it be that firms have more in common with the legendary Woodstock Music Festival of 1969 than the caricature of the monolithic industrial empires that are so often portrayed as villainous? They do, but I should put one adjective in that description; *successful* firms have a lot in common with Woodstock. Great, iconic companies like Honda, Google, or Apple, the best restaurant in town, a brilliant stage production, or a successful local retailer are fabulous mixtures of a great idea and superior execution.

First, it takes the great idea. Then, hopefully, lenders and investors recognize it as such and add their capital; managers properly interpret the concept and make it real; talented workers buy-in and add their sweat and talent day-in-day-out; and customers see the final product and love it such that they become loyal patrons and spread the word to others. Subsequently, for a brief time, maybe a year, maybe ten years, there is a great coalition that makes all those employed in the venture as productive as they can be by giving clients exactly what they want and then some. It's a festival; a magical moment when all the pieces fit just right.

It usually doesn't last forever. Workers mature and move on, tastes change, ownership needs to monetize their investments as they age and their needs change. Maybe the company sells, maybe it drifts too much, or maybe consumer tastes change. In a process called "creative destruction" coined by the transcendent economist Joseph Schumpeter, new products, services, and technologies improve upon their predecessors such that they destroy the prevailing market for and value of older, now inferior products, thus always forcing innovation and improvement. And such great innovations are often serendipitous happenings, bringing together just the right mix of financial capital, physical capital, and human capital, no matter where they might be found around the globe such that a product or service is produced that adds significant benefit to the lives of consumers, even if it comes at the expense of yesterday's outstanding company.

Polaroid was once a happening; Atari was once a happening; Snapple was once a happening! In the same way that someone thought of having a concert in a farm field in upstate New York, and it was the right choice of performers and the right moment and hundreds of thousands of people showed up, and all involved created a legendary experience—a great coalition of human capital, physical capital, and financial capital can coalesce to create greatness! Is a Woodstock that much different than Apple releasing the iPhone and people lining up around the block in city after city to just be a part of it? Moreover, is it evil that the iPhone destroyed the value of some other competing phones that it transcended? Hardly. Society as a whole is made better by innovation driven by consumer demand. Is it a painful process that requires us to all work harder as not to become obsolete? Well, considering that we trade time at leisure for time at work with the hope of yielding the highest value possible, the answer is an emphatic "yes"; innovation is incredibly stressful requiring us to work harder than we otherwise would like. But that's a bit of the magic of the Econosphere.

By naturally routing capital to its highest uses, this holistic system does not reward one individual at the expense of another; rather, it seeks to make the whole run as efficiently as possible. This process means that we as individuals are rewarded to the extent that we contribute. If we contribute to the production of goods and services that are experiencing relative declining value as demand wanes, then we ourselves will be motivated to produce different kinds of outputs that are more highly valued by society, thus increasing the overall value of the output produced within the Econosphere. In real life, that likely means changing jobs to find better opportunities at another firm or on your own—maybe you go out and start a firm that will be better than the one you just left!

Often times, perhaps sadly, that process of you and others leaving the firm might well be the death knell for that firm. For a moment, maybe several years, there was a great collaboration producing a great product; then another firm figures out how to do it better or cheaper; and then the collaboration begins to break down. Capital leaves for better returns elsewhere; workers sense stagnation and look for other opportunities. And that might be it for the firm, and as it withers, it makes way for the rising competition. The firm is dead! Long live the firm!

My Job Is Nothing Like Woodstock

Still, when it is 6:30 a.m. and you need to get your butt out of bed, travel forty minutes on two busses, and open up the cell phone accessory kiosk that you have to man by 8 a.m., this all might sound like a big load of crap, for lack of a more descriptive term. So, let's talk about why *you* do it.

Several generations ago, you might not have found yourself in such a predicament. Although the Econosphere's laws are forever unchanging, its nature drives us to change our situation through innovation. And, the innovation that has taken place in recent centuries has clearly required us to all work more cohesively and collaborate. It was not all that long ago that the majority of workers in the now-developed world were farmers, and in many cases, subsistence farmers. That is to say that a household owned or rented a plot of land, and their major occupation was producing goods and services for themselves. They grew and tended much of their food. They tended animals that provided eggs, milk, and meat, not to mention transportation and labor. They grew vegetables that could be canned and consumed throughout the year. They built and maintained their own shelter. And yes, there was trading with others as well. A household could buy, say, a plow, or a stove, certainly cloth for the creation of clothing, but work was much more immediate in that you actually did eat what you produced, and you went hungry when things at work didn't go all that well.

So why did this change? An argument could be made, I suppose, that life on the farm beats life at the cell phone accessory kiosk via the 439 bus that picks you up, give or take 30 minutes, at 7 a.m. at the corner of York and Main. Just imagine, you could be feeding chickens and have a hat and suspenders, and eat nothing but fresh produce all day long!

I would counter that, come February, when you are looking at another delicious meal of jarred tomatoes and salt pork, your warm stool at the kiosk and lunch at the food court with its copious specialties and ingredients hailing from around the world might sound darn good. Look at it from the subsistence farmer's point of view. Ask the guy who tries to keep his drafty shack warm in the middle of winter with whatever firewood he can stockpile, "How would you like to sit here on this nice stool and sell this stuff to people who walk by, and for lunch you can have a nice plate of kung pao chicken costing less than what you will get paid for just an hour's worth of work?" I'm guessing he'd like the sound of that, though you would have to describe to him exactly what is kung pao chicken—he's been eating primarily jarred tomatoes and salt park for quite awhile.

You see, there is no way that our subsistence farmer, on his own, would be able to design and manufacture cell phone accessories, not to mention compile all the ingredients necessary to make kung pao chicken. At some point, our subsistence farmer was lured off the farm and into a job where he could specialize so that he could be more productive. As opposed to trying to supply everything he and his family needs, some of which he was good at producing, and many things he was not all that good at, he found that he could work a job and produce just one or a few things and earn the money necessary to purchase goods from other people similarly specializing. If he made only, say, carriage wheels, he could buy flour from the miller, meat from the butcher, clothes from a clothing store, rent an apartment from a landlord, and so on...and have a larger basket of goods for his household to consume. He might even get weekends off! Well, our former farmer is no different from you.

Heck, you could try to produce everything you consume. You could grow your own vegetables, have a few chickens, make your own clothes, build your house, create your own entertainment, and make your own wine. And I'm willing to bet that one or more of these things you may just do as a hobby, but what the vast majority of us find is that we are more productive when we specialize, thus allowing us the resources to actually have a bit of leisure time during which time we can, say, garden in our backyards or on a balcony just for the joy of it.

You Are a Specialist!

So how do we specialize? We specialize by collaborating with the creators of great ideas, suppliers of financial capital, managers who see the process through, and fellow workers who all specialize in their chosen fields. If you think you're a great pharmaceuticals salesperson, for instance, you don't go and try to manufacture pharmaceuticals! After all, you don't know how to manufacture pharmaceuticals! You go find a job at the best pharmaceutical company that you can! You find the one with the best ideas, the most research capital, the finest manufacturing processes, and the best branding. You align yourself with the people who make the best product as possible. What you do is join a firm!

It is a great thing when you think about it. Of course, hopefully you are a good pharmaceutical salesperson; otherwise, the great people at the best firms will not want to align themselves with you; they will find someone better! I know that sounds cold, but this dynamic only makes you either improve your sales techniques or find another specialty. Otherwise, you will be working at a not-so-good firm, pushing inferior products and likely not being as productive as you would otherwise care to be. That's the tough love of the Econosphere. The Econosphere provides the incentives to push people and resources to their highest uses; you just need to keep your eyes and mind open so that you can read and accept the signs. Goods are not the only things that are assigned a price; even your time on this earth is assigned a market price. It's your chore to find the industry, firm, and occupation that maximizes that price (keeping in mind also the relative costs incurred in one job versus another, of course—you might take lower pay at the phone accessory kiosk than for the manure shoveling job).

But How Should We as a Society Look at a Firm?

We should look at a job at a firm as our opportunity to specialize and be productive. We should see firms as serendipitous intersections of ideas, capital, and labor. When we find a good thing, we should enjoy it and work hard to keep it a good thing. And when it is no longer good, we look around to find a better opportunity. Such is life in the Econosphere. It sounds straightforward enough, I think, from the point of view of the individual. After all, all the value in the Econosphere comes from the individual during his or her lifetime. The economy springs forth from you; you make decisions for yourself; the individual's point of view is the key vantage from where decisions are made.

Why do we as a society seem to care so much about firm-level events, as if the firm were the single unit of output as opposed to the hives of individual effort that they are? There are so many mixed messages. We love our jobs, we love our brands, but we sometimes seem to be at war with the owners and management of firms, particularly when there are changes or job losses. Why would the U.S. government want to bail out GM or Bank of America as if they had a vested interest in the brands? Why would we choose to look more highly on some companies than others? And protect some from foreign competition and let others out in the wind to twist? Moreover, why is there such a negative connotation applied to "big business"? Heck, we don't even like "corporate farms"—those nice people who grow and raise most of our food. Firms are wonderful, amazing things, and just about everything we have in terms of goods, services, and technology is the product of these serendipitous coalitions. It's odd that we seem to dislike those at the helm of our most successful firms—after all, small businesses do not graduate to big businesses without being good at what they do.

So where is the love? Maybe there's too much love! Maybe all the incessant, highly addictive branding and marketing makes us love our favorite brands and firms so much, we think we own them. You might love Budweiser so much that you were incensed that someone was selling your favorite beer to some foreign conglomerate called InBev! Perhaps you and your fellow longneck drinkers thought that you could and should stop this theft of your brand from the evil foreign conglomerate! But you couldn't.

You as a drinker of Budweiser can choose to drink Budweiser or not, but you don't have any say in management whatsoever. Budweiser was a public company and management works for the shareholders. If a majority of shareholders want to sell, then sell they will!

Maybe that sounds sad, but it is fair. It is investors who put their capital at risk in the venture. I'm sure they appreciate you the customer, but their investment is expected to make returns for the investor, and has little to do with your own feelings of ownership. Of course no company can afford to tick off their customers; otherwise, they will not remain a going concern for the future, but that is the new owners' problem, now isn't it?

Remember, a firm is a happening. Founding principals want to make a great idea a reality. Investors look for great ideas in which to invest. Workers gravitate toward well-conceived, well-capitalized companies where they can maximize their productivity, and consumers are the ultimate beneficiaries of an inspired product and service. But when an investor needs his or her money back, that may be it for the company as we know it. Really none of the parties are married to each other forever. Management could leave, important workers could leave, or the founding principals can cash out. Even Ben and Jerry eventually sold out to Unilever! And in the case of those U.S. automakers who have recently run aground, it was the customers who had had enough and split.

So how do we explain it when, say, the government steps in to support one firm and condemn another? It is hard to explain. Does the government sometimes love a firm so much that it is willing to put taxpayer dollars at risk to support it? Probably not. More often than not, it seems that government steps up to support firms to retain or create jobs among their specific constituents. Thus, they intervene on behalf of workers, which does seem odd considering who actually owns a firm. Workers don't own the company, and they can come and go as they please. The workers typically get paid for services rendered, and thus they have little at risk other than their personal investments in their particular community—housing, schools, relationships, and such. In some cases, the death of a firm does greatly impact the financial health of a community and the value of its assets.

Considering that, I think we could very well conclude that government may intercede in corporate affairs not on behalf of anyone directly involved in the enterprise. Rather, those times when government involves itself is likely in defense of the value of the physical assets owned and used by workers of the firm, not to mention the tax revenues that spring from these enterprises. One does not necessarily save, say, GM because people love GM cars or policy makers feel bad for the ownership. Rather, policy makers want to keep voters in their homes and keep the physical towns, buildings, and businesses viable to retain votes and support tax revenues.

That's the difficult thing when it comes to brick-and-mortar assets. They cannot be moved in most cases, so as the Econosphere shifts resources from industry to industry and location to location, and the people follow the changing economic winds, the physical assets are at least temporarily left empty and nonrevenue-generating. And, if you think about it, governors, representatives, and senators are a lot like buildings. Their constituents may cross state lines in their ongoing effort to maximize their happiness, but the senator cannot change the geographic confines of his or her jurisdiction. If firms fail and are not replaced, politicians can become relics in the same way as do empty storefronts and abandoned buildings.

What does warm the heart a bit in this otherwise unhappy tale, however, is that it shows that policy makers are real flesh and blood people, just like us. They are utility maximizers, and they do what they think is best to support their own situation!

All that said, I would say that policy makers seeking to support failing institutions are barking up the wrong tree. It is better to foster innovation than to protect a crumbling past. Entrepreneurship and high-quality labor are what keep some states perpetually ahead of others. Hanging on to a cherished firm that has seen better days is, in many ways, self-defeating. As we know, firms are serendipitous happenings that often come with a limited life span. There is no point in clinging too tightly too them; otherwise, one is impeding on the process of creative destruction and the Econosphere's role in helping capital find its highest use.

You might argue that if a policy maker were to, instead, support those initiatives that made their state particularly friendly to entrepreneurs and investors, that supported the kinds of education that produced talented and creative workers, and generally set the table for firms to emerge, flourish, and fade over time according to changing tastes and technology, that might be the way to maintain residents and high asset values. That kind of understanding requires an appreciation for the Econosphere, how it works, how it finds the highest uses for resources, and how it works to help us all maximize our own happiness. Propping up a dying firm, in comparison, is certainly unproductive, if not a bit morbid. There is a reason why we bury our dead.

Sparkle and Fade

Firms are our own creation. They are relationships that we create based on our own selfish interests. We all want to maximize happiness. Many of us do this either by creating a firm, investing in a firm, or working in a firm. Certainly, the firm cannot exist for much of a duration if it does not produce products and services that people are willing to trade for. So even consumers are a part of the equation, though they hold no equity per se. We might hope that these relationships last a lifetime, but we should not expect them to, nor should we be too offended when they do not. They are moments in time in our long ascendency toward greater sophistication.

For instance, technology does not stand still. Some firms are flexible and aggressive enough to keep up with new technologies, but they are the exception. Many firms explode onto the scene with a great initial product or service but are subsequently trampled in the stampede of others hoping to improve upon that first foray. You might have loved your classic Atari 2600 4 Switch Woodgrain System, but its displacement by the Nintendo NES 101 Top Loader was part of maximizing our utility with better technologies. Imagine if policy makers tried to save Atari in the same way as they intermittently try to save Chrysler or GM. It would have been foolish to do so in the case of Atari; otherwise, we would likely still be playing Space Invaders; one wonders if we are guaranteeing suboptimal cars in the future by trying to save failing car manufacturers from the competition today.

Brands are great. Firms are great. But people are what matters. It is the human life span that creates value. Sure, great brands and the firms that own them are a big part of harvesting that value. But when those brands are no longer great, they play a much smaller role in adding to aggregate wealth. We should not worship firms or brands as permanent deities; rather we should view them as great accomplishments in human cooperation and entrepreneurship, and realize that often when these firms fail, it means that others are succeeding.

A firm is a moment in time; the Econosphere is forever. We need to feel more passionately about the Econosphere than we do about any particular firm, whether we love it or hate it. The firm exists because the Econosphere provided the incentives to bring ideas and capital and labor all together. The firm exists because of the Econosphere, and it cannot exist without it. Remember, the Econosphere is our social environment, and if our environment wants to impose extinction on something, such as the dinosaurs or AIG, we should not question it. Remember what happened in *Jurassic Park*? Or how about *Frankenstein*, for that matter?

6

Stupid Policy Tricks

I guess we need to hit upon the two-ton elephant in the room at this point; we should spend some time discussing government and its role in all of this. So far, we talked about this wonderful social biosphere, our economy, and how it guides our lives by providing incentives, often via market prices, that aid us in making the best possible decisions with the information and abilities that we have. But what the heck does all that have to do with, say, former Treasury Secretary Hank Paulson and Fed Chairman Ben Bernanke appearing on television with apocalyptic warnings that unless a bank bailout is passed before the end of the week, the economy as we know it will cease to function? Where does a panicked, wild-eyed Treasury Secretary speaking with the full authority of the United States government fit into this otherwise somewhat hippyish view of the Econosphere as a perfect system bigger than any one man's concerns? Tragically, it doesn't fit very well, but we can't deny its presence. So, let's talk about it.

Why So Cynical?

The government is an interesting entity. Before we dissect it, I do think we need to admit to ourselves that it exists. Government exists! Governments exist all over the world and have existed throughout history. Society almost always creates a government. So, citizens must see it as a necessity, and a good thing to have. Otherwise, they would neither create a government nor support one.

Now, what is government good for? In other words, what was government created to achieve? Today, that is a complicated question. Government permeates nearly every facet of our lives in one way or another. It taxes, it regulates, it judges, it coaxes, it lectures, it distributes, it redistributes, it attacks, it defends, it catches us when we fall, and it pulls us down when we stand. There is, seemingly, no end to its charter. It is the solution to every problem, and when its solutions inevitably create their own unintended problems, it is the solution to those problems, as well. Yet, it exists, and it must exist for a purpose.

Does that sound cynical? I think it might, and I apologize.

Let me explain my mindset today, and perhaps why I am infected with a fit of cynicism. Yesterday, I was a passenger on the Acela Express train between New York and Washington. I am a big fan of the Acela because it is so much more pleasant and convenient than flying between the major cities along the East Coast. From DC to New York to Boston, the Acela has become the preferred mode of travel for many business people and policy makers. And yes, I have even shared a car with Vice President Joe Biden during his famous commutes between Wilmington and Washington DC.

One of the interesting things about the Acela is that many groups of travelers sit and work around the tables in the cars, and you cannot help but hear their conversations (unless you are in the quiet car). It's a bit like a bar without the loud music. If you listen, you can hear all that you need to know about the Mid-Atlantic economy and culture.

A few years back, I distinctly remember listening to a relatively young guy; I think he said he was a recent medical school graduate, yammering on rather loudly about the several hedge funds that he had founded and was running, and the several Russian models and tennis pros that he was dating. It was at that moment that I knew the bull market was in trouble! Wayward medical doctors who serial-date Russian "models" should not be managing money at the farthest reaches of the risk curve.

The topics discussed on the Acela are always changing depending on what is hot in the economy. Over the years, it has gone from dot-coms to home flipping to hedge funds and structured products to biotech and recently on to the harvesting of federal bailout and stimulus money. And it was yesterday's overheard discussions that did turn me a bit cynical. I am writing this chapter amid the ramping up and administration of several emergency programs, TARP, TALF, PPIP, the stimulus bill, the omnibus spending bill, and God knows what else. And there was only one topic of conversation on the Acela yesterday. The topic du jour was prepping for meetings with government bureaucrats in hopes of getting a piece of the billions of dollars that Washington is planning to push out into the economy. Just in my area of the car, I overheard constituents of firms in alternative energy, medical research, and a very large, well-thought-of international nonprofit for whom I have now lost much respect based on the discussions among the scheming posse that they were sending to the capitol that day.

Perhaps the only person riding the train who did not fit that mold was a chubby, kind of shiny, 30-something staffer who was on his cell phone discussing to whom "he and Tim" were planning on doling out money—the denominations were in tens of millions of dollars, as you might imagine. He was very pleased with himself, and all I could think about was the fact that that money represented time and energy that could have been spent elsewhere by those who created that value, but was instead diverted to the whims of this gentleman and his colleagues. Those people who created the value that that money represents had no say when that money was taken through taxes or borrowed on their behalf, nor do they have a say in how it is spent. However, the pudgy, shiny man-boy seemed to have a rather large say. People need to create value to procure funds to spend and save; the government need only take money through the force of law to get what it wants, and there is no necessity for or presumption of value creation on the part of these takers whatsoever.

Needless to say, I got off that train not feeling very good about the state of public policy. Believe it or not, it was, in fact, a great treat to be back in the New York subway upon my return. Although many of the problems that these programs seek to fix have their beginnings in New York, when I looked around that subway car, I didn't see anyone brushing up their PowerPoint presentations in hopes of getting a cut of someone else's hard-earned wages; I just saw individuals on their way to and from creating goods and services that are appreciated by their fellow people, and people looking forward to getting home and spending time with their family and friends. There were far fewer professional panderers, near as I could tell.

Protector of Property Rights

I hope that little diversion helps explain the somewhat cynical tone of this chapter thus far. It is just that by spending several hours in transit with people whose sole purpose is to ask for someone else's money, which was taken from that someone else or borrowed on behalf of that someone else by an entity with a self-proclaimed right to take or borrow what it wishes, gives one a sense that something rather large is polluting our beautiful Econosphere. And yet, as was stated: Government exists. It has almost always existed through history; it is created by people, is supported and maintained by people, and thus must be a beneficial thing. And through all the diversions and transgressions that we find on government's to-do list, there is one special, central purpose that it is here to fulfill. There is only one thing that government has a true mandate to accomplish, and that is to protect property rights.

If you boil down government to its marrow, it is there to make sure that someone does not stroll across your lawn, conk you on the head, and claim your property as his or hers. Certainly, you can say, I don't need government to do that. I can take care of my own stuff! Or at least, I can hire someone to take care of it. And yes, you could. But, if everyone were to hire their own security force to protect their own property rights, it would be certain that differing ideas of property rights would flourish simultaneously and create ongoing conflict, such as in, say, Somalia, Afghanistan, or in the Godfather movies. Thus, developed societies all eventually see the value of just one set of property rights and agree on one unified body to maintain that code of law, and that, my friends, is your government!

Now, you may say, "My government does a lot more than that." You might point out that your government sets emission standards for autos. Yes, but I can counter that those emission standards are there to protect the quality of the air that is breathed as a public good shared among us all. The government is protecting your access to clean air; it is protecting your property rights. You might point out that your government sets safety standards for food. Well, yes, but those standards keep companies from taking your life via harmful ingredients or poor quality; and as we know from our study of the Econosphere, your life is your most valuable property. You might point out that your government sets education standards. Well, in that case, it might be a stretch, but you might conclude that someone with a high school diploma is less likely to crawl through your window at night and steal your television set, or is less likely to cause damage to public property, which costs everyone both in terms of loss of use of that property and in paying the cost of fixing the damage. What of our expensive national defense? Well, that keeps foreign aggressors from coming in and taking all our stuff. You see, this is what government does. It upholds laws that detail what is theft and what is not.

All the high-minded rhetoric boils down to that basic fact. This is government's useful purpose. As you go out there into the Econosphere to create value and support yourself and your family, the government is there to make sure that you can keep the rewards of your labor.

Unfortunately, the government often tries to do more than just that. And generally, I might add, that as its well-intended or otherwise-intended programs stray away from this central purpose of protecting property rights, these programs become difficult to pass or maintain support for. There is a reason why legislation favoring, say, more favorable treatment of unions—at the expense of nonunion workers, investors, or consumers—or transfers of wealth from one group to another are not very successful in the long run. They have nothing to do with protecting property; they have more to do with the redistribution of property. Subsequently, there is a hint of theft in the policies that cause some to rightfully rail against them. Moreover, such policies run against the nature on the Econosphere itself. These public efforts on our behalf make us not only run less efficiently, but also ultimately lead to all kinds of unintended consequences.

For instance, government bans on the production or importation of some good can create black markets for the banned item. Those involved in these informal markets operate outside the bounds of accepted law or codes of conduct such that these shadowy elements are more likely to commit crimes and abuses against one's property and one's person. There are many times that society stops to ponder what is worse, the banned item or the resulting crime that can occur as a consequence of said item finding its way to market via criminal elements.

The Government Is Nelson

Now, it is not my intention to simply dwell on these issues of governing. First and foremost, I want to give you the ability to see the government as a player within the Econosphere. But how does one grasp the many tentacles of people, buildings, equipment, statutes, statues, and so on that are spread through every corner of society and in all places around the world?

Thankfully, government is made up of individuals who are its workforce, and we can always understand their motivations, just as we can understand our own. Each of these individuals is a utility maximizer, encouraged and nurtured within the Econosphere. Every government official is a government official because he or she believes, taking into consideration his or her abilities and the information at hand, that a government vocation will maximize his or her own happiness. Even when our elected officials use their preferred lexicon of "public servant" to describe their post, they are still utility maximizers, just like everyone else. They are there for purely selfish reasons; and there is nothing wrong with that—some for love of power, some for love of helping people, but they are all there based on their own personal agendas.

As a consequence, elected officials and their staff can be expected to do the same sorts of things that all of us do to keep our positions and get ahead. In the case of our public servants, this may mean working at funneling as many government resources to the benefit of those who support, fund, and vote in favor of them. That makes perfect sense. Also, public servants need to be mindful of their post-government careers, which often entail utilizing their familiarity with those in government to represent private interests. They often go on to be hired as lobbyists, board members, consultants, and the like.

Given the vast amount of money collected and spent by governments, an ability to act as a bridge between private concerns and public coffers is a valuable thing indeed, such that the rewards can be great. Moreover, these types of actions, vocations, and strategies all fit well within the Econosphere's system. People try to find where they can be most productive so that they can maximize utility, procuring what they need while also preserving free time for enjoyable pursuits. Life as an influential public servant with a subsequent well-paid stint in the private sector makes exceedingly good sense.

However, our point here is not to ponder the individual pursuits of politicians, I want you to consider government as a whole. A government is similar to a firm, the motivations of which we have already discussed. However, it's not quite the serendipitous, temporary moment that is a great firm. Firms can go out of business rather easily if they fall out of favor with their customers. In the case of governments, it's quite rare that one will actually go out of business, save for the occasional coup. Sure, elections can switch out the individuals in office and the party in charge, but the government as an entity will remain. Not only will the government remain, but also its power to legislate, prosecute, tax, consume, and acquire is almost permanently intact. A firm is a temporary entity, but government is more or less forever.

In particular, its revenue sources are permanent. In all developed countries, it is illegal to refuse to pay your taxes. Thus you are a permanent client and a captive contributor. In that sense, the government is kind of like the big bully on the playground who can demand lunch money from the smaller kids. Moreover, after that lunch money is procured, it can be dispensed in any way the bully wants. Government acts as an individual with a limitless credit card or a limitless supply of nerds to shakedown, spending where it wants, consuming what it wants. As such, I like to think of government as just one really big person; kind of like a big bully who knows how to get what it wants. In this sense, I like to picture government as a giant version of Nelson from the Simpsons.

That really fits for me. I don't think government is evil; and on the Simpsons, Nelson has definitely shown his softer side and at times has almost been a sympathetic character. That said, if Nelson wants Millhouse's lunch money, Millhouse is going to have to cough it up. This power makes Nelson his own man. He feeds his own wants, follows his own path regardless if that path might trample upon someone else. Yes, government is just a big, giant, loveable yet intimidating version of Nelson. And as an aside, you don't want to make an enemy of Nelson. It's generally safer to do what he says.

Stimulus

Now, our friend Nelson, that is, the government, does try to help us from time to time by "fixing" the Econosphere when we don't like the message that the Econosphere is telling us. Often times this comes in the form of countercyclical programs during recessions, or in another name, "stimulus." There is fiscal policy, controlled by the elected branches of government, and also monetary policy, which is handled by the less political (usually) Federal Reserve Bank. The Fed is perpetually conducting countercyclical policies via its open market committee (FOMC), either trying to tamp down growth that is above potential, or ramp up weak growth, all under the two-pronged mandate to foster price stability and full employment. They typically do this by targeting short-term interest rates by pulling money in and out of the banking system...essentially affecting the price and amount of capital available for borrowing. More recently, the Fed has expanded its range of actions to include...well, anything and everything. The Federal Reserve's balance sheet has now become a repository of all manner of financial instruments taken as reserves to bring greater liquidity amid an ongoing financial crisis. As of the writing of this book, it is uncertain whether this unusual strategy will prove transitory or a new permanent model for conducting monetary policy.

The Fed, at its best, is independent from the executive and legislative branches of the government, taking a detached, bookish demeanor. This waxes and wanes depending on the era and who is in charge, and, many politicians and a few Fed Chairmen have shown by their actions that they were never true believers in the traditional nonpolitical role of the office. For instance, the Fed under William Miller during the Carter Administration acted as an arm of the Executive branch to very bad effects. Chairman Greenspan testified before Congress during the Bush (George W.) Administration regarding political matters such as tax cuts, and more recently, Chairman Bernanke has worked in lock-step tandem with the Treasury in the latter days of the Bush Administration, and with the Treasury under President Obama. On the other extreme, Chairman Volcker, who brought what I might call an "I'll See You in Hell!" style of monetary policy, completely sank the economy and the reelection hopes of President Carter for the purpose of restoring price stability. Volcker is now looked upon, and rightly so, as a near-mythic Fed Chairman who was completely impenetrable to political influence.

The nice thing about monetary policy, from the point of view of one who loves the Econosphere, is that it is somewhat indiscriminate, not particularly singling anyone out for favorable or unfavorable treatment. Moreover, if the Fed primarily looks after price stability, that is, defending the currency as a store of value, then that is a win for all of us. We typically store our saved earnings in either our currency or assets denominated in our currency. If the Fed is there primarily to make sure that that currency is a good and safe store of our hard earned wealth, that helps everyone and makes the Econosphere more efficient. So that's a good thing.

Aside from this, monetary policy is generally looked upon as the most effective way to manage the cyclicality of the economy. On that front, however, I'm not all that sure. The Fed clearly has not ended the existence of business cycles; booms and busts are still with us. Moreover, there is somewhat specious reasoning when it comes to "proving" the effectiveness of monetary policy. When the economy booms, the Fed increases interest rates, and then when the economy wanes, the Fed will decreases interest rates, and it goes on like this. Many economists look at that and see causality where the economy is speeding up and slowing down at the behest of the monetary policy. I would like to think that I am a pretty good theorist and econometrician, and, well, I'm just not that convinced.

Think about it. The economy booms, the Fed increases interest rates, then the bubble bursts, and the economy decelerates or contracts. Did raising interest rates cause the economy to decelerate, or was monetary policy just along for the ride and absolutely ineffective in slowing the economy before the inevitable economic imbalance gave way? Similarly, when the economy is in recession, the Fed always lowers interest rates. During this period when rates are low, the economy otherwise does its thing and repairs what imbalances had developed, and inevitably begins to grow again. The Fed's lower interest rates are invariably given credit for the rebound. But I just don't see how one can assign causality. This is just policy along for the ride. I'm sorry, but I give all the credit to the Econosphere!

I Am the Sun God!

How do I know this? Well, I know this because I am the Sun God! That's right; kneel before me, for I control the sun! Every morning, I wake before the sun comes up. Then I make a cup of coffee, face the window, I utter the magic sun summoning phrases, and do the sun summoning dance. Inevitably, the sun does rise. You see! I control the sun. Bow down before me!

Seriously, if you are willing to believe that the Federal Reserve has the power to avoid or end recessions, you should also be willing to believe that I control the sun. You can see a correlation between monetary policy and the business cycle, in the same way that you can see a correlation between my sun ceremony and the rising of the sun. If you are also willing to assume causality and conclude that monetary policy exacts control over the business cycle, using that same reasoning, you must also conclude that my ceremony causes the sun to rise. Are you willing to do that?

All that said, I don't see any harm in monetary policy per se, as long as interest rates are set with an eye for inflation risks. Moreover, and I think this is perhaps a very big point, there are millions of people who do not believe, as we do, in the Econosphere and its capacity to steer incentives so that we can provide for ourselves. For these non-believing folks, it is comforting to believe that the economy is controlled by wise, old central bankers in gray suits that meet in a big marble building in Washington DC. They are essentially modern-day priests of the temple, but instead of sacrificing animals, they are setting interest rates. I would much rather that people believe in themselves and in the function of our self-correcting, self-directing Econosphere, but if old guys in gray suits talking in tongues about interest rates make people feel better, than who am I to try to wreck that relationship?

Council of Wise Men

Aside from monetary policy, even more fun, and disturbing, is fiscal policy. What is fiscal policy? Fiscal policy is elected officials spending great gobs of your money to fix the economy on your behalf. This person has a little too much money; this one doesn't have enough; so we'll take some from this one and give it to that one. This industry doesn't have enough capital, so we'll take some from this one and give it to that one. And whammo, the economy is fixed; the recession is over!

There are a few prevailing theories about fiscal policy. Much of it is built upon the writings of John Maynard Keynes, an economist who seems to go in and out of fashion depending on how the economy is performing. When the economy is faltering, and calls for policymakers to do something are loudly voiced, Keynes is inevitably exhumed. To summarize the relevant Keynesian points, Keynes did not believe that the economy naturally reverts back to full-employment. He believed that the economy could potentially, if not probably, arrive at a sustained pace of growth well below optimal levels. As such, it takes a council of wise men to redistribute capital in a manner that is more suitable to achieving peak performance in the economy. Left leaning parties around the world tend to fall into the Keynesian camp, as these parties primarily seek to comprise that council of wise men. However, these days, even right-wingers are apt to call for "fiscal stimulus" in conjunction with loose monetary policy during crisis, creating essentially an unholy mish-mash of diametrically opposed economic theories that likely have both Keynes and Milton Friedman spinning in their respective graves. Those who founded the schools of thought supporting either fiscal stimulus or monetary stimulus were not close bedfellows whatsoever; such that, ordering up both in the same breath is the intellectual equivalent of sauntering up to a bar and ordering a gin and milk.

Regardless of the theoretical problems, it is often just the details of the policies themselves that create all sorts of

havoc. Remember, government is like a big giant Nelson—
that is, a big, maybe well-intentioned, perhaps starved for
love, but often misinformed bully. Anything it does will create a large effect based purely on its size and reach alone,
and one must expect reverberations throughout the system.
You are essentially introducing an alien force into the
Econosphere that is not wholly governed by the Econosphere's natural laws. As a result, there will be ramifications; if it helps to picture a scenario, you might recall the
movie *Invasion of the Body Snatchers*. In the 1978 version
with Donald Sutherland and Leonard Nimoy, the world
ended up relatively orderly as the soul-destroying aliens
sapped the individuality out of every man, woman, and
child. The movie ended there, but given what we know
about the body snatchers and the rules of the Econosphere,
I would predict a resulting lack of innovation that would
have eventually led to a declining standard of living for the
alien invaders, not to mention extreme boredom.

Beyond the broad problems of fiscal intrusion is that it
is not a generalized intrusion, as typically is monetary policy. It often targets particular important voting groups, or at
least certain demographics that are thought in need of stim-
ulating to get the economy going. In that case, think of the
various tax redemptions or stimulus payments that have
taken place over the last decade. The government sends
low- and median-income families a check in the mail; and
the hope is that these checks will unlock a torrent of economic activity. Instead, usually, it just sets off a round of bill
paying and television purchasing that roughly equals the
face value of all the checks. It is nothing but a transfer of

money from one group (or one generation in the case of federal borrowing) to another. Where is the value-add in that? Don't bother looking for it; it's just not there. And as you might recall, the only way to create wealth is to add value; it is a mystery to me why it has become a political consensus that shifting money from one group to another is a means to create wealth.

Here's another one of my absolute favorite pieces of fiscal stimulus. Remember the Jobs and Growth Tax Relief Reconciliation Act of 2003? Of course you don't! Let me refresh your memory; it was George W. Bush's stimulus package for the recession following 9/11. Actually, there was a lot of good stuff in that one, including decreases in several tax rates that have lasted thus far, though the future does not look bright for these measures given our rising federal debt burden. Nevertheless, why I bring this act up is that it had a great piece of silly stimulus within. It allowed for temporary accelerated depreciation and increased expensing of capital investments. Sounds good, right? The idea is that by making the accounting rules temporarily more favorable, capital equipment orders would rise and that would create jobs and "jump start" the economy.

Well, it worked, sort of. Capital equipment orders responded. But is that a job creator? Consider what capital equipment does before you rush to answer that one. Computers, machines, manufacturing robots, and the like are explicitly a substitute for labor. Capital investment allows labor to become more productive through the use of technology, thus in the near-term, these items actually reduce the need for additional labor. This piece of stimulus actually sweetened the incentives to reduce the labor components in the production process, and will forever be a big part of what history remembers as "the Jobless Recovery." Certainly it was not this act alone that caused the jobless recovery; ongoing outsourcing to China and India also played a role there, and the advancements in information technology that would have taken place regardless of the act; but nonetheless, if you want someone to hire people in large numbers quickly, you don't make it explicitly less expensive to go out and buy labor-saving equipment!

Redistribution: In Search of "Fairness"

Most fiscal policy intends to redistribute capital to strike a balance that will either re-accelerate the economy, or at least make a poorly performing economy more palatable for key supporters. This redistribution takes place in all sorts of ways, person to person, industry to industry, generation to generation. Even the relatively benign loosening of monetary policy explicitly shifts interest payments away from savers in favor of lower costs to borrowers. There is no free lunch, as economists are fond of saying! In the case of policy, which is not a direct component of wealth creation, if you favor one, you take away from another.

Sometimes, the scenarios become almost bizarre. Take, for instance, the recent bailouts of certain banks and the U.S. automakers. If customers, lenders, or investors pull capital out of an institution because of their poor management, the U.S. government then acts to nullify that penalty by putting money back into said institution. In the case of the automakers, car buyers choose not to buy a certain brand of car, and the federal government turns around and puts taxpayer money into said automaker to make up for the lack of sales. Now, there are details in all these things that make these moves more explainable. Somewhat dubious arguments about institutions being too big to fail, systemic risk, and extenuating circumstances outside of a carmakers control are made. Nonetheless, the Econosphere will relentlessly shift capital to its highest uses to make the entire populace as a whole as productive as possible. Fiscal policy that redistributes that capital is the equivalent of trying to reverse the course of a river. It's costly, not particularly useful, and in most instances, highly unlikely to be successful.

More frequently, there are simply programs designed to move money from one demographic to another. Often, this is punitive to savers and investors, and favors people who consume much of their income. On one hand, these folks can use some extra money during tough times, as they have no real cushion should their income stream stop or shrink. Established programs such as unemployment insurance are excellent platforms for such efforts to keep income flowing. They are broadly supported because everyone pays into the pot of capital.

Other programs are less palatable: programs that take tax dollars to mitigate home foreclosures, changes in the tax codes to subsidize some and not others, and so on. For instance, I've always wondered why the tax code rewards people for having children or people who take out large mortgages. Doesn't the government like childless renters? I guess not. Moreover, because children use public services, shouldn't parents pay more in taxes? I don't have anything against parents with mortgages, I'm just pointing out the obvious inequity.

These items are baked into the tax code on an ongoing basis, but during times such as these, there are typically sweeteners that pass additional savings onto the favored taxpayers. If you are a winner in these events, you're happy. If you are a loser, you are not. But that is almost beside the point. The question is, how do these efforts improve the economy? In so much as they redistribute what the Econosphere has already distributed, they run the risk of making the economy operate less efficiently, not more efficiently. And that is the key! The economy must run more efficiently for a recession to eventually turn into a recovery.

One thing that has always struck me as a bit odd, especially seeing that I am an economist, I've never been quite sure why it has become a consensus that it is better to give money to people who will spend it than to let it stay with people who will save it. I realize there are input/output tables and other such devices, and perhaps somewhere, sometime someone has calculated multipliers that claim that consumer spending holds greater value than consumer saving. But does anyone believe that? Particularly now that we are trying to recapitalize banks and free-up capital for lending, how in the world is it better to take money from savers and give it to spenders? Some ideas are so silly that the only way they persist is by becoming such accepted dogma that no one dares question them. My suggestion to you would be to question anything and everything about public policy intended to improve the Econosphere. If you want to improve balance within the Econosphere, do what you can to restore it to its unfettered natural state. Moreover, the market is perfect; it is information that is imperfect. If you want to improve the results of the market, you must improve information. Constantly changing the rules to shift capital to favored industries and demographics actually obscures information.

Barriers to Trade and Prosperity

The other large piece of policy that is often debated during tough times is trade policy. The Econosphere loves trade, in that we all trade our time and talents with others' time and talent in our pursuit of maximum happiness. The Econosphere cares nothing about national borders. We all have time and talent, and it should all be used to the benefit of everyone regardless of nationality.

However, some hold different views, and for understandable reasons. Trade can rob a person or a town of its major vocations, and that is devastating. The Econosphere perpetuates such difficult outcomes because these outcomes improve everyone's lives as a whole, but that improvement on an individual basis might be miniscule in comparison with the personal and absolute losses of, say, a manufacturing worker or a manufacturing town that has seen its major employer disappear. Problems are also exaggerated when nations have different profiles. Although it is true that nations that are different from one another benefit the most from trading with one another, as each provides different kinds of goods and services. In the case of an exporting country that allows polluting industries or low wages, a company following the rules in the United States would rightly point out that it is hard to compete.

This is a good point. But let me give you another way to look at it. We here in the United States chose to live under certain rules. Many of the developing countries that we trade with choose to live under a different set of rules, often because their concerns are more primal, such as just feeding everyone. There is little you can do about foreign labor and environmental standards save for refusing to consume products and goods that are sourced from areas where you do not support prevailing environmental and labor laws. That's fair enough, and I think those types of selective consumption decisions are appropriate.

But also consider this; think of a country that subsidizes the production of goods that they trade with others or a country that is willing to tolerate relatively worse labor conditions or looser environmental rules. They are actually willing to help subsidize another country's consumption! Why would they do that? There are a few common reasons, such as reaching full employment, but I would argue that none of the reasons make any sense whatsoever in the long-run. They rob themselves of the value that they are creating and may endure harsher conditions that yield themselves less utility. But in the meantime, before they come to their senses, it is a bonanza for consumers in the importing country! It's not very smart policy on their part, but if it means that you can drive a cheaper car or buy a less-expensive garden hose, well, you can make the judgment whether you want those things or not.

Still, changing trade flows more often than not happen outside of policy decisions. Even without subsidization or other political maneuvering, relative advantages between different nations shift over time. And sometimes, industries appear in one nation, and disappear in another. This is a natural part of the Econosphere and involves individuals choosing to do the things that allow them to be most productive. In the end, as long as these shifts in occupations and industries are allowed to happen, the Econosphere is most productive and operating as smoothly as possible—efforts to stop this natural process can allow for pressure to build such that it can yield quick and violent shifts when the pressure gets too great, such as what we saw in the economic and subsequent political collapse of the Soviet Union. But aside from the most dramatic extremes, just the action of protecting one industry not only robs us of a bit of our collective productivity, it also explicitly takes a little away from everyone and gives it to the protected domestic players. That may be politically palatable, but let's be clear about what is happening. The government is taking a bit from a lot of people and injecting that capital to help a small number of people. Why does the government like those few people more than they like those who are net losers in this arrangement?

With this in mind, my broader point in the case of stimulus is relatively plain. In the case of trying to jump start an economy, there is no apparent benefit, quite the contrary, of either robbing consumers of their preferred sources of goods or of transferring wealth from the many for the benefit of the few.

7

Ten Ways to Maximize Wealth and Happiness for Yourself and Everyone Else

We are a part of an immense, sustainable social ecosystem that provides us all the incentives we need to best utilize our single, important raw material: Our own inborn potential and ability. We deplete this raw material over the course of our lives for the betterment of ourselves and those for whom we care, during which time we produce the goods and services that better all mankind. In the same way that our physical environment provides food, air, water, warmth, and more for an array of living organisms so that it is a self-sustaining system, our social ecosystem, our economy, is the mostly invisible counterpart to the physical environment providing the incentives that we need to successfully interact with one another and prosper.

Mankind has wrought great harm onto our physical environment over the centuries. And now that we are, perhaps, a bit more enlightened as to our effect on the natural balance of things, we aim to repair those problems that we have created and avoid making those same mistakes in the future. The Econosphere is in much the same shape as the physical environment, but we have yet to become fully enlightened as to the ramifications of our actions. Because this social environment is more difficult to see and monitor, and because we have not yet trained ourselves entirely to feel, appreciate, and accept its role in our lives, we have not yet had our environmental epiphany as it pertains to our economy—our Econosphere. There is an Earth Day, but there is no Economy Day!

But like any new movement, progress starts with a step and builds upon itself with each additional step. If we keep taking those steps, we will eventually look back and see just how far we have come. Below are ten markers along the personal journey I hope that you will take to first, maximize your own utility so that we all benefit from your time and talent, and second, bring awareness and stewardship of the Econosphere up to the standards that we now apply to our physical environment. Eventually, we will not only help ourselves, but also knock down the man-made impediments that keep so many people around the world living in poverty, not reaching the full potential innate in their only important raw material, their own humanity.

1. Know That It All Comes from You

For goodness sake, stand up and know that everything you are and everything you create comes from you! The belief that one's wealth and well-being is somehow ladled out to each of us by the powers-that-be is a sad thing indeed. We see ourselves as net-consumers, adrift on the sea without oars, or like a pack of rats fighting for every morsel. We treat ourselves like we don't deserve what we gather for ourselves and our family. And it is absolutely preposterous that we do so.

Everything is borne from the individual. Wealth is generated by the harnessing of our own human lives and abilities. We are the ultimate renewable resource. Nothing has any value without us. Oil is not valuable in the ground. Gold has no intrinsic value. Land has no value. It is when we extract, transport, refine, harvest, and utilize these resources that they hold any value whatsoever. It is the sweat of our brow and creativity of our ideas that create value and wealth. It's not doled out to us. It springs forth from us like oil from a well. If you think back to the rhetoric of elections past, you might remember one candidate or another promising what he or she would provide for the voters, when all the time, it is the people who provide everything! It is the people who create the value that will be taxed to pay the salary of the elected official! The wealth flows in the opposite direction of what is implied.

Now, with this knowledge, there also comes some responsibility. You have a basic ability to create value, and that is what will sustain you your entire life. But it is up to you to make the best of it. If you want to improve your lot in life, it often requires the aggressive pursuit of education and training. It might also require flexibility, creativity, and mobility. Say, if one profession becomes relatively less valuable or a city loses its chief industry, it is implicit upon the individual to find other ways to add value and produce goods and services that are valuable to others, which might mean a change of vocation or a change of location. That's your responsibility to figure that out.

Your goal is to maximize your own happiness. You might wish that you could spend your entire life on the beach sipping margaritas. However, supply is finite, and nothing is free. You need to keep on your toes so that you can trade for all the things that you need and desire while also saving time for the pursuits that you value, such as time with family and friends. To do that, you need to follow the Econosphere's signals and find those places and industries where you can maximize your potential and thus maximize your own happiness.

The good news is that you're already doing this; it is inborn within you. Even better news, fully embracing this impulse will mean that you will not only be taking charge of your own situation, you also will become aware that you are the source of your own well-being, and subsequently you will not be ashamed of your success when you achieve your goals, and you will not be lost for direction during those times when success is scarce.

2. Love Your Environment; Be a Price Hugger

I am sure that you are familiar with the term *tree hugger*. It refers to people who love their environment so much that they want to protect it. They love it so much they hug it, and I suppose a tree is about the easiest thing in nature to get one's arms around. It also conjures up the images that we have all seen of people protecting forests by attaching themselves in some way to the trees that someone is seeking to cut down.

It is a nice image, to see someone who cares so much for something that they will drop everything, and even potentially put their own well-being at risk to protect what they love. Well, I am hoping that you will start looking at our economy as something that you want to love and protect. The Econosphere is what sustains you and provides you the signals and incentives that you need to create the goods and services that are most needed and desired, both locally and around the globe. It does this primarily through market prices.

Things that are scarce and highly desirable are assigned high prices; things that are plentiful and not as highly appreciated are assigned low prices. As we look around to find those things that we can produce and trade to sustain ourselves and our families, it is these prices that help us see what is most needed and where we should concentrate our time and abilities. Consequently, market prices are vitally important to all our well-being! If we didn't have them, we wouldn't know where to concentrate our time. We might spend our lives producing things of little or no value to our fellow man. As a result, I tend to think of the Econosphere equivalent of being a tree hugger as being a *price hugger*. We should love market pricing in the same way that an environmentalist loves a tree. Without trees, we would not have shade, oxygen, building materials, and so on. Without prices, we would have nothing to guide our productive lives! Please, please be a price hugger!

Today, being a price hugger is as important as it has ever been. There are ongoing efforts to artificially set, change, and obscure prices in our Econosphere, and these efforts will make us less prosperous. There are public policies put in place to make fuel cheaper, raise pay for certain occupations, subsidize certain industries, create tariffs to increase prices, and provide more goods through public programs so that individuals are never aware of the actual price of what they are consuming! These policies are a thick haze obscuring our vision and muddling our incentives. Someone in power is assuming that he or she knows the true "value" of something more so than does our Econosphere. Policymakers might believe that a few people can better value items than can billions of people making billions of individual judgments. Similar arrogance at one time led people to blow up mountains, clear-cut forests, divert rivers, and try to remake our physical environment into something closer to their own personal vision of utopia. We learned hard lessons as a result of this type of willfulness, and we are reaping the same bad harvest by trying to reassign market prices to better fit someone's personal sense of value.

If I can impress upon you just one thing, it would be to learn to love market pricing. Market prices tell you something that no other indicator can. It tells you what the world needs and where you can do the most good! There is almost nothing else in the world more important than that one thing. Without it, we are lost. Please be a price hugger!

3. See No Thieves

Begin to embrace that value springs forth from you and every individual, and that the prices that you and everyone else receives in return for your efforts reflects the relative supply of and demand for the goods and services that you produce and trade. Clumsily dancing on a street corner might yield a cup full of spare change. Inventing a new high-tech surgical tool that can save many lives yields a more handsome take. Most of us produce things that generally fall somewhere in the middle of that range of values.

The point is, if the Econosphere is allowed to function as it should, people will be rewarded based on the value that they create and bring to others' lives. This is a truly wonderful, fair, democratic, existential thing. We should be inspired by and aspire to the heights of those who are truly productive in their occupation, yielding great value from their lives. We should not, however, allow ourselves to become paralyzed with jealousy; something that is not entirely easy to do. We can find this calm place where we are not vengeful toward those who are successful by remembering this one central point: All value springs forth from the individual. Your wealth comes from you; what you have does not come at the expense of another. An unfettered Econosphere is never a zero-sum game.

Now sure, you might point out that some people inherit their wealth, and I would counter: So what? Inherited wealth is nothing more than stored labor from a previous generation. It is a wonderful thing if someone can produce

so much value to give future generations additional comfort. There is no theft in this either. The creators of the
wealth are perfectly within their rights to pass on their
stored labor. The incentive to provide for future generations keeps us productive late in life when some might have
already created enough to live comfortably through the balance of their own life spans. Grandpa could have lain on the
beach during his last twenty-five years on this earth; wasn't
it a wonderful thing for the world that he didn't? Instead,
he chose to remain productive.

Choose to aspire, but not envy. Just because someone
has wealth, does not mean that he or she has acquired it by
taking it from someone else. As a society we have laws
against theft. It is not theft to create valuable goods and
services that the world craves; at least it is not considered
theft yet!

4. Live Without Borders

Look around; do you see any natural borders that man
cannot or should not cross? I see no barrier that has not been
overcome by hard work and the innovation of mankind. Yet,
when I look at maps, I see nothing but artificial lines—barriers drawn by who knows who, who knows when, for who
knows what purpose!

These lines have horrible consequences! On one side
of a border, you may find plenty, prosperity, and freedom.
On the other side, you will find poverty, conflict, and hopelessness. These lines have no natural meaning, but the

differences in conditions on either side of these lines have great meaning. In almost every case that I know of, on the side of prosperity, we find the Econosphere flourishing, setting prices, allocating resources, and incenting workers. On the other side, we find corruption, strife, castes, central planning, and public monopoly. We do not find a system where the market sets prices, we do not find individuals with the freedom to acquire skills and choose their own vocations, and we do not see the ability for the individual to own or acquire wealth. This is what these artificial lines create.

The Econosphere cares nothing for those lines; it knows only that it works best where left to operate according to its natural laws, and that it will operate far less equitably where the few and powerful try to supplant its influence. In this vein, and like the Econosphere, I might suggest that all of us live paying as little attention to these lines as possible.

Certainly, love your country and honor it. Moreover, work to affect change where people are suppressed or treated unfairly. However, outside of these imperatives, trade freely with the other inhabitants of the Econosphere, in which we are all fellow citizens. It is through this exchange of time and talent that we all can support ourselves, prosper, and maximize utility. Turning away from that exchange does both a disservice to you, in that you deprive yourself of potential trading partners and the full variety of goods and services available to you, but you also partially deprive others of their means to earn a living and support themselves in a manner that reflects their potential.

Any artificial line drawn across a map that restricts the free trade among fellow citizens of the Econosphere is the social equivalent of a locked gate, fortification, or dam restricting freedom of movement itself.

If you are to experience all that can be experienced in this world, you must trade with all corners of this world. If we hope to increase our own living standards and everyone else's as well, we must allow all people to be as productive as they possibly can be.

See no borders. Trade freely and prosper, and subsequently those who trade freely with you will also prosper.

5. Many Brains Working on Small Problems Beat Few Brains Working on Big Problems

In every life there are many, many challenges. The Econosphere is a self-sustaining natural system, but it is not nirvana and we are certainly not free from problems. The Econosphere is a system for the equitable distribution of scarce resources. But those resources are still scarce! Moreover, consumer demand over anything but the shortest time horizon is essentially limitless, so there is a lot of demand that goes unfulfilled given our finite resources.

Moreover, we have our information problems. The market is perfect; information is imperfect, and as such, we all make mistakes. It is these sorts of mistakes, made on a grand scale, that cause volatility in the economy, such as when we have speculative bubbles and subsequent recession.

And so we naturally want to avoid these problems. We don't like to see people lose their homes. We don't like to see people lose their jobs. We don't like to see people live in poverty. So we want to do something.

The one thing that I want to put across is that no one person, or one group of like-minded people, knows the answer to every problem. But maybe, if we can put all our heads to work, and each of us work on those problems that we know best, we can make this world a much more pleasant place.

With that in mind, I believe that we should all vigorously question attempts made by one person, or a few people, to solve our biggest issues. This is the folly of central planning. No one person, or council of wise men, can know everything. Can one small group of people who do not know you personally have any idea what car *you* should drive, or how *you* should spend, save, and invest *your* money? Moreover, how can one group of generalists know how the banking system should work, know how to dole out healthcare, pick and choose what goods should enter our markets, and have an educated opinion on how *you* should raise *your* kids, what *you* should eat, and how *you* should best spend your time? That is asking too much of anyone! And for anyone who might think that they are up to that task, I believe that he or she may think too highly of his or her own abilities.

Rather, look for micro decisions made on a micro scale to solve our greatest problems. Some might say that most people are not savvy enough to make such decisions on their own, but I would argue that no one is savvier about how to spend his or her own life span than the individual who knows his or her situation the most intimately. Time and again, we may be told that the individual needs help, but just think of the billions of people who manage lives, families, and businesses all on their own each and everyday.

Just as an example, we are told that people cannot manage their own financial obligations. Yet, every time interest rates decline, millions of people make the individual effort to refinance their debt. That takes savvy, and yet, these ordinary folks who are deemed not worthy to manage their own affairs make sure it gets done quickly and efficiently.

Just like everyone else, I don't have all the answers, nor do you. But when the call is raised for someone to come and solve our biggest challenges, I would argue and hope to convince you to not look for a wise man to solve your woes, look to yourself and everyone else to make the tough decisions in those personal areas where each of us are the only real expert. Many heads are better than one. And many heads, each working to solve those problems that they are closest to, are better than a few heads trying to solve problems with which they have no intimate knowledge or expertise. This is a central tenet of the Econosphere, and if followed, would certainly lead us away from some of the foolish decisions that we have made in the past and may well make again in the future.

6. Solve Your Information Problem

So with that in mind, if we are to be the ultimate decision maker within our realm of knowledge, if we want to make the best decisions possible so that we yield the best market outcome, we need to solve our own information problem. The absolute best thing that you can do for the world is to be the most knowledgeable, trained, and skilled person that you can possibly be. You are in charge of you and yours, so we need you to be successful! If you achieve this, and everyone else does the same, our aggregate wealth and well-being will rise sharply and relentlessly. It is that simple.

As such for your sake and everyone else's sake, make the most of the education available to you. Seek out additional education and training. Never stop learning. Read and stay up on topics. Just think of the pain and loss that we could have saved ourselves had more mortgage borrowers during the recent housing boom been better aware of the terms of their contacts, the likely trajectory of home prices, the fact that home values can actually fall, and had a realistic grasp of their future income stream. This knowledge would have not only made the recession less deep, it also would have eliminated it entirely. Moreover, what if mortgage-backed securities investors had taken more time to understand what it was that they were buying? They wouldn't have been left with empty investments and massive losses.

These sorts of information problems are at the basis of all our economic problems. For policy makers, if they want to make the economy run smoother, they could and should find ways to improve access to and the quality of education— even if that includes a significant increase in private educational facilities. Just think what could have been avoided had everyone taken a personal finance course in high school! Moreover, there should be a serious attempt to make markets more transparent through the creation of better, clearer data and analysis.

Our problems are solvable. First, they need to be solved on a micro basis, empowering the individual. Second, they need to be made with the best possible information available. If you want to improve the outcome of your decisions, improve your information!

7. Preach the Word

Now, I must ask your help to further the mission that I have taken on by writing this book. Now that you...

> Know about the Econosphere...
>
> Know that you are the source of the value created in this world...
>
> Are comfortable with the way that market prices and trade help guide us and allow us to support ourselves...
>
> Know that what other's have, they have created and not taken...
>
> And know that it is our information problem that plagues us, and that each individual must strive to get better information so that all peoples' lots in life can be improved...

...I ask you to spread the word.

Spread the word not because I want you to, but because the more people that understand, the better chance we have in saving, maintaining, and restoring the natural state of the Econosphere. The more people that understand the Econosphere, the more price huggers we will have, and the less likely they will be to support oppressive regimes that hold themselves high as the source of our prosperity or who want to suppress the Econosphere in favor of their own system of distributing resources.

I sometimes stand back and marvel at what the environmental movement has accomplished over the last few decades. The idea of associating oneself with being "green" and concerned with the natural environment is near universal now. Imagine what could be accomplished if we could do the same with awareness of the Econosphere. We would drastically reduce poverty and oppression and give hope to those who do not realize that value flows from within them, and that the human life span is the primary raw material that they will use to support themselves throughout their lives as they attempt to maximize their utility, that is, happiness.

At the very least, do it for yourself. The more people who are out there with a keen eye on adding value and producing the goods and services that are demanded, the more likely you will be in finding good value in trading your time and talent. There could be a tremendous amount of pent-up demand unleashed throughout the globe if only the Econosphere were allowed to flow freely and guide its citizens to become more productive with their lives.

8. Have a Healthy Fear of Your Public Servants

And for those who might claim that you don't have to do it yourself, that, perhaps, you might be a victim, or you deserve better, and for those who promise that they can deliver to you what you want in exchange for your support, be very, very skeptical.

I certainly do not want to send you into your backyard to start building a bunker, or send you off into the woods to become a survivalist. However, I do think it behooves us all to always be skeptical of government efforts to extend their reach into the Econosphere. As we discussed in Chapter 6, "Stupid Policy Tricks," because the government as an institution sits outside of the rules of the Econosphere, it tends to behave differently than do firms and individuals. Individuals might go broke and starve if they cannot find a productive way of living; firms can go belly-up if their goods or services are unwanted; but the government will always have the right to tax, and is thus highly unlikely to go out of business. This "immortality" for lack of a better word changes its incentives.

Don't get me wrong, support your government and honor its role in maintaining the rule of law and defending property rights. This role is conducive to building the kind well-function countries that now flourish throughout the world. However, also know that all value and all wealth spring forth from the individual, not from the public bureaucracy. As such, when someone in a public office promises that he has a way to increase wealth by tinkering with the Econosphere or by adjusting incentives, know that this is simply a transfer of wealth away from one person to another. And know that the Econosphere is the system that helps us best direct capital and resources. It seems far-fetched to believe that one person or one group of like-minded people are better adept at directing the flow of capital and the allocation of resources than the collective wisdom of billions, each working in their own areas of expertise!

What is the primary incentive of the public bureaucracy? Among the most compelling, I believe, is to increase its importance by increasing its sphere of influence. This is done by grabbing additional tasks and responsibilities, and by also increasing its budget to reflect these new roles. The larger the budget, the greater the responsibility, the more necessary and influential the bureaucracy and its leadership become. Absolutely none of this has anything to do with maximizing *your* utility.

Don't dislike your government. Certainly, be a proud supporter of democracy and of all the wonderful things that it has brought to the world. But at the same time, be proud of your role as an individual who creates wealth to support yourself and your family. Know that your incentives are different from the incentives that drive a bureaucracy. Know that the bureaucracy wants to grow. When it does expand its reach into allocating resources and directing investment, not only does it cause the Econosphere to function inefficiently such that it decreases aggregate wealth, it becomes hard to push back into a smaller, less intrusive role.

Anytime someone in an elected office claims that he or she can do a better job of running the economy than can our own natural Econosphere, be very skeptical.

9. Rise Above the Fads

As with hemlines and the color of kitchen appliances, the opinions of economic pundits and political figures wax and wane with every cycle. Rise above it! The laws of the Econosphere are fixed. No matter if we are in a recession or whether we are in an economic boom, you will always be a utility maximizer, and the Econosphere will always be allocating resources to its highest use. Market prices, which take into account all the information that is publicly available, will always be the best indicator of relative value.

This never changes. Sure, we may not like the market outcome. We may mourn a firm that disappears, a region that is sharply impacted by a secular downturn, or the loss of our own wealth. However, these occurrences are the result of imperfect information, not an imperfect Econosphere. If we need to fix the problem, we need to improve the information.

Retooling our economy at times of crisis is often akin to saying, we need fix nature: Let's put the ocean over here; we need to repeal the law of gravity; let's put wild elephants in Canada; and we need more komodo dragons in Brazil! As if that would fix our problems! We would just end up with a lot of dead elephants and komodo dragons.

We can no more improve the Econosphere than we can improve upon the laws of nature. But what we can do is concentrate on operating as efficiently as possible within our social environment. We need to allow prices to freely adjust, allow trade to flow unfettered, allow for excesses to be reduced and deficits to be replenished. Each person needs to see that he is the source of his own wealth and find those things that he can provide that will yield a high value so that he can maximize his own happiness.

It is never the case that capitalism was okay for this decade, but now socialism is the way to go, that is until communism makes more sense, and then after that maybe we'll dabble in feudalism, and maybe then a little anarchy. We have one natural system. It does not matter what you call it, who approves or how fashionable it is. We can allow it to guide us, or we can try to extinguish it; one of these options leads to the best possible outcome, the other is quixotic and inevitably leads us down a path toward poverty, corruption, and inequity.

10. Spend Your Lone Raw Material Wisely

All this brings us back to you, the individual. You are born with your own loaf of bread. How big that loaf is depends on whatever abilities you have, the degree to which you can augment that ability with education and training, and the degree to which we as a society allow the

Econosphere to provide incentives so that you can maximize your potential.

You have one goal and one goal alone: to maximize utility (that is, happiness). What makes you happy is unique to you, but it will typically comprise some portion of your time spent at work, producing goods and services to be traded so that you can attain the goods and services that you desire, and the rest of your time spent at leisure, pursuing activities that are not necessarily of any value to the market place, but are valuable to you. Within this framework, you may end up being a workaholic bachelor with a sports car, a fire-fighting husband and father of three, an actress and international jet setter, a small business owner, or a Red Cross worker in Africa helping those who are in great need. It is all up to you.

It is your life, and your life is your chief raw material. It is yours to spend, and you are the best expert in deciding how to spend it. No one else can do this job better than you—not the government, not the council of wise men, not the pundits, not a Hollywood celebrity, not even an economist—you are the expert. Embrace the job! Know that the guidance that you need is provided by our free economy and its market prices. Know that you are the source of your wealth. Know that to make the best decisions, you need the best information possible.

Protect the Econosphere from those who want to impair it. Seek out the education and training that you need so that your time is as valuable as it possibly can be. Realize that your purpose on this earth is not to work the hardest but to maximize your own happiness. Stop and smell the roses when you want to; concentrate on producing something of value when you need that additional wealth.

Be as happy as you can be, and live unapologetically—the economy comes from within you. You create your own value; it is yours to spend how you wish.

INDEX

W–Z

FINANCIAL TIMES

In an increasingly competitive world, it is quality
of thinking that gives an edge—an idea that opens new
doors, a technique that solves a problem, or an insight
that simply helps make sense of it all.

We work with leading authors in the various arenas
of business and finance to bring cutting-edge thinking
and best-learning practices to a global market.

It is our goal to create world-class print publications
and electronic products that give readers
knowledge and understanding that can then be
applied, whether studying or at work.

To find out more about our business
products, you can visit us at www.ftpress.com.